On Top
of
Glass

My Stories as a Queer Girl in
Figure Skating

On top of Glass

KARINA MANTA

Alfred A. Knopf
New York

THIS IS A BORZOI BOOK PUBLISHED BY ALFRED A. KNOPF

Visit us on the Web! GetUnderlined.com

Educators and librarians, for a variety of teaching tools, visit us at RHTeachersLibrarians.com

Library of Congress Cataloging-in-Publication Data
Names: Manta, Karina, author.
Title: On top of glass : stories of a queer girl in figure skating / Karina Manta.
Description: First edition. | New York: Alfred A. Knopf, [2021] | "This is a Borzoi book published by Alfred A. Knopf." | Audience: Ages: 12 and up | Summary: "A memoir of Karina Manta, the first female member of USA Figure Skating to come out as queer."—Provided by publisher.
Identifiers: LCCN 2020044001 (print) | LCCN 2020044002 (ebook) | ISBN 978-0-593-30846-2 (hardcover) | ISBN 978-0-593-30848-6 (ebook)
Subjects: LCSH: Manta, Karina—Juvenile literature. | Women figure skaters—United States—Biography—Juvenile literature. | Bisexuals—United States—Biography—Juvenile literature.
Classification: LCC GV850.M35 A3 2021 (print) | LCC GV850.M35 (ebook) | DDC 796.91/2092 [B]—dc23

The text of this book is set in 11.25-point Gamma ITC Std.
Interior design by Andrea Lau

Printed in the United States of America
October 2021
10 9 8 7 6 5 4 3 2 1

First Edition

For my dear friends
Lindsay, Mackenzie, Natalia, and Rayna.
And for Hayley, who is only absent from these particular
stories because she was busy at swim team practices.

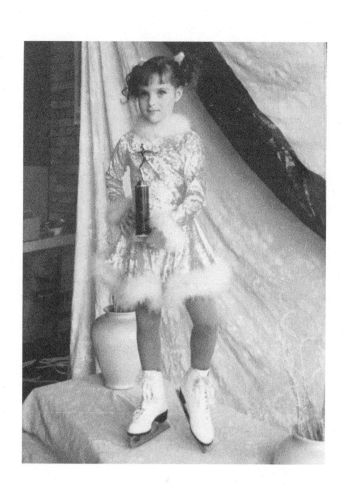

On top
of
Glass

In Defense of Spoilers

I am the kind of person who ruins endings.

Before I watch movies, I look up their summaries online. I allow my friends to reveal the best plot twists from their favorite TV shows. When I make attempts at cracking jokes, I go straight for the punch lines. I have been known to flip to the last page of a book before I even read the first. Worst of all, when I tell stories, I can't help but give some bits away too early. I am a menace in the face of suspense.

Maybe it's because I have a desire to feel in control. Maybe it's because I'm anxious. My mind likes to busy itself with worst-case scenarios. I just always want to know—to confirm—that things will be okay in the end.

Can you blame me?

The first time I googled the words *lesbian figure skater,* I was a young teenager. I sat at my parents' desktop computer. I opened a new tab in incognito mode, and I clicked the keyboard quietly, even though I was home alone. My initial search didn't conjure any names. Instead, I found a couple of forums that speculated over the sexualities of several athletes—nothing concrete. I altered my search: *bisexual female figure skaters.* Still nothing. I revised again: *gay female figure skaters.* Google offered me a list of men.

I changed the search entirely: I looked up *bisexual politicians,* and I looked up *bisexual Supreme Court justices,* and I looked up the word *bisexual* alongside every career I ever thought I wanted.

At the time, I didn't know what I was looking for. I was sure that I was straight. Positive. I thought I was just scratching an itch of curiosity.

These days, I know better. I can see what I was trying to do: I was trying to look up another ending—an ending to my own story. I was seeking answers to questions that I was too afraid to ask out loud: What could my life look like? Was my existence even possible? I grew up without knowing a single lesbian in real life—or any queer women, for that matter. While I scoured the internet that day, I looked for hints at who I could become; but after tapping through pages and pages of search-engine results, I didn't manage to unearth even a single clue.

For some, the thrill of the unknown might have been exhilarating, but I was not the kind of person who found adventure in uncertainty. I was the kind of person who ruined endings.

I shut down my browser, and I told myself to forget about the investigation. I told myself to stifle the itch. For years, I felt untethered.

Here is the first spoiler of my story. I already warned you—I can't help but give little bits away too early.

I could never bring myself to stop searching. The keyboard clicks ingrained themselves into my muscle memory. My hands typed and tapped again and again. I spent countless nights online, trying to make sense of my world—trying to find proof that my story could have a happy ending . . . or proof that I could exist at all.

For a long while, my situation seemed grim.

But slowly, as the years passed, a trail of names began to appear during my late-night investigations. With persistence and time, I was given a list. I came across the names of my heroes, and the names of my friends, and the names of a few brave strangers from all over the world—I found a community and a history that had been hidden. And eventually, as I scrolled along the list, I was able to find my own name. A little blue hyperlink. A buoy thrown to my younger self across the internet's void.

If you are someone who needs to be assured, I can assure you: Things will be okay in the end.

1

The Very Beginning

March 20, 1996. Sometime around one or two in the morning.

My story starts at a hospital in Olympia, Washington, on a day that I don't remember. I imagine the hospital was like any other: cold, white-walled, punctuated by the sharp smell of cleaning supplies. I imagine my parents were taken to a stark room, detailed with pink balloons. Maybe my mother's hair was pulled back into a ponytail. Maybe my father tried to crack a few jokes to ease the tension.

From the stories, I know that the doctor almost didn't arrive on time. My older brother's delivery took hours of painful coercion. My mom swears she broke her tailbone during the whole process. But I arrived quickly—eager to experience my first bittersweet breath. I arrived so quickly, in fact, that my grandfather, who was a surgeon, almost had to deliver me right on the spot. But luckily, my mother's actual doctor made it just in time to catch my squirming body as I made my grand entrance into the world.

I imagine I screamed. It must have felt good to test the capacity of my tiny lungs.

The staff members at this particular hospital were accustomed to birthing plump, pale babies with slippery bare skin. I've been told that most of the babies in the neighboring bassinets came out bald as can be. That explains everyone's surprise when I arrived: small, writhing, and . . . fuzzy. My body was covered in dark, wispy hair. I had a crown of black curls atop my head to match. I'm told it's fairly common for babies born a little premature to find themselves covered in hair, but I must have been an exceptional case (I can probably thank my father for that—I have his especially dark hair).

"Wow . . . look at all that hair!" a nurse exclaimed. I imagine her tone suggested more than surprise—maybe even the tiniest, slightest shade of judgment.

My father immediately took offense and decided he and the nurse were bitter enemies. *How dare they make fun of my daughter?* he thought. He probably even grumbled out loud.

I imagine I screamed again. This time with a purpose.

The point is this: My body has been an issue my entire life—starting from my very first seconds in the world.

~

After my abrupt arrival, my parents gave me a name: Ana Karina Manta.

My first name was a gift from my paternal grandmother, Ana Maria. My middle name was passed down from my mother, Karin. My last name—as you might have already assumed—came from my father.

Inside the hospital, my parents whispered my name with soft, cooing voices. The vowel sounds carried the consonants like they were riding the gentle swish of a rocking chair. I was so small, and my thoughts were too fresh and young to be considered typical thoughts—but if I had known what music was, I probably would have thought my name sounded something like music.

My legs would have kicked in response.

~

As my tiny body grew, the power of my lungs seemed to dissipate.

I was a quiet child. Quieter than most. I was the kind

of toddler who constantly hid behind the reliable barrier of my mother's leg.

Some of my earliest memories are from preschool—I can picture the modest classroom and the rust-colored playground—but inside these memories, there are no sentences. No words.

My parents enrolled me in a Spanish-immersion preschool because they wanted me to learn the language that my dad grew up speaking (my father was born in Uruguay, a small country in South America that borders Argentina and Brazil), but my mouth rejected language—English and Spanish alike—so I mostly said nothing. I became an observer. I held my stories very close to my chest. I played alone in a corner of the playground, tightly clutching the plastic hand of a Barbie doll.

I am pretty sure my thoughts might never have found a way out had my mom not picked me up from preschool one dreary afternoon and driven me to a dance class at a local rec center. My older brother, Luis, immediately ran to the center of the gymnasium floor to join a circle of other children. Several young women arrived, pushing strollers and carrying diaper bags. The teacher stood up front, wearing primary colors and an exaggerated smile.

I imagine I hid behind my mother's body at first. I can only assume the other children looked on incredulously.

But then everyone began singing songs, and I noticed a waking in my bones—an irrepressible kind of joy. The instructor elicited sweet, rainy sounds from a tambourine, and I worked my way into the circle of other children. I danced. From the stories, I know that I didn't hold back. My usual timidity morphed into something new.

Although language often failed me, movement did not. While dancing, I didn't seem to need sentences or words. While dancing, my body was not the problem anymore. It was the answer.

When I turned four, my family moved to Chandler, Arizona.

There were five of us by then: me, my parents, Luis, and my younger brother, Marques. We'd been living in the Pacific Northwest, so my dad jumped at the opportunity to take a job somewhere with a little more sunshine, and Arizona seemed like the perfect place.

Winters in Chandler were hot. Truly hot. The kind of warmth that called for the rumble of air conditioners at noon; the kind of warmth that craved ice water when none could be found frozen atop all the backyard pools; the kind of warmth that smelled of sunscreen tucked into the pores of every kid who grew up in the state (a smell that I swear stays on Arizona children forever—even after they grow up and scatter across the globe).

In elementary school, the elusive "snow day" was not

an event of anxious anticipation but instead a mythology. The kids who moved to my hometown from northeastern states whispered legends of early mornings spent listening to the local news. I remember a singular moment during kindergarten when the classroom thermometer dropped below the infamous freezing point of thirty-two degrees. I watched the windows until the bell rang in hopes that the one solitary but mighty cloud in the sky that day would bring us all a few flakes.

Around the same time, I was invited to a birthday party at a local ice rink. I was five years old. I wore a purple zip-up hoodie because, like most desert-raised children, I didn't own any heavier coats.

I was still a reserved child. Parties made me nervous, and this party was no exception. My shyness didn't mix well with the sugar rush of other children unwrapping presents and sucking the helium from balloons, so I kept to myself.

As the other kids raced to grab skates, I hung near the back of the line. When I got ahold of a pair—probably small enough to slip onto a doll's feet—my mom helped me tie the laces tight against my ankles.

By the time I made it onto the ice, its glassy surface was dusted with a layer of snow that had been kicked up by the other skaters. The powder was rich, bright. The color of whole milk. I had never seen anything like it. I watched my feet skitter along, struggling for stability in a new, frictionless world.

An older girl spun in the middle of the rink, where an area had been blocked off with cones for the real skaters to practice. A boy in hockey skates maneuvered around the cones and then attempted to jump over them in a death-defying stunt. He nearly toppled into the spinning girl, but she didn't even notice. She just kept spinning. It was magic. It was almost as if her movement had created a new kind of weather—something that the rest of us could watch but couldn't feel.

My mom clutched my shoulders; she kept my balance steady while I teetered across the ice. I was not very graceful, but I imagined I could be. Movement on the ice somehow made sense. Wobbling around the rink gave me that same kind of joy I'd felt at my very first dance class, but with more speed, more freedom, and more cold wind against my face.

The other partygoers eventually tired of skating. They unlaced their boots, ran off to play arcade games. But I didn't mind being left alone. I stayed on the ice as long as I could. I only exited the rink when the Zamboni honked, telling us all that it was time to go home.

When I took off the skates, my feet were aching and swollen. I inspected the damage: a pair of blisters kissed the area just above my arches. I poked at the bubbles. I was tempted to see how much pressure they could withstand before they burst. The blisters stung, but while I was on the ice, I had barely noticed. This was probably a sign: Even at five years old, I loved with an intensity that was blinding and dangerous.

After the birthday party, I begged my parents to sign me up for lessons. They were understandably wary: I had been pretty terrible at skating. My mom's arms throbbed from the hours of holding me up. She didn't want to turn one exhausting afternoon into a weekly habit. Plus, she had already enrolled me in ballet classes, and gymnastics classes, and a season of soccer, during which I insisted on wearing my dainty pink ballet shoes while I ran around the field. (I was the family anomaly—the only sibling who was not a die-hard soccer fan from birth.)

Despite my parents' hesitation, I remained persistent. I kept begging for skating lessons throughout the springtime.

By summer, they struck a deal with me: If I spent a few weeks practicing on a pair of Rollerblades, they would sign me up for some actual lessons.

The following days of summer passed with unwavering consistency.

I woke up late in the mornings. My mom sliced oranges and grapefruits from the trees in our backyard, and my brothers and I ate them at breakfast—dumping sugar over their tart wedges, pouring too much milk into our cereal bowls. Then we raced outside. The summer air smelled like citrus and cows—in those days, my hometown was still half made up of farmland. It was the kind of summer that suburban kids wait for all school year.

While my brothers scraped their knees on scooters and careened their bikes off the edge of the sidewalk, I practiced rollerblading around our cul-de-sac. I stayed outside for hours, baking under the sun until my skin pickled. I tried to twirl like the spinning girl at the rink. Mostly, I fell. But I kept practicing. Within a matter of days, I grew bolder—making a ramp of our driveway, racing my brothers on their respective sets of wheels. I was hooked.

My parents kept their promise. After a couple of weeks, they signed me up for skating lessons.

In the midst of a desert summer, I took to the ice—a quiet, cold little girl who had found an unexpected home.

The "hobby" stuck, probably longer than anyone expected it to. I spent a short lifetime circling one rink after another. I spent years chasing a storybook version of winter. I fell in love with a peculiar and extravagant sport.

The sport was not always kind. Sometimes my body felt more like a problem than a solution. Sometimes my vision was clouded by rhinestones and hair spray. Sometimes I wondered why I stayed—but skating gave me a means of expression that I spent my whole life struggling to grasp.

Because of skating, I finally learned to fish my own stories out from beneath the ice.

Here they are.

2

Tiny Heart Attacks

Heart disease is the leading cause of death in the United States.

I'm pretty scared of death, so naturally, I am afraid of a lot of things that could cause death: snakebites, pharmaceutical side effects, plane crashes, undiagnosed STIs. But mostly, I am afraid of heart disease because it is the *leading* cause of death.

The fear started in elementary school PE.

My PE teacher was like most elementary school PE teachers: She had a loud voice, and she wore an array of colorful T-shirts that she had acquired by participating in local benefit 5K runs. She was wearing one of those

T-shirts when she called the class together for an announcement.

"This month, we are going to be preparing for Jump Rope for Heart," she explained. "On Valentine's Day, everyone will take part in a jump-rope-a-thon, and we'll raise money for the American Heart Association."

Initially, I was on board with the idea. I loved jumping rope—I could even double-Dutch pretty well. As with figure skating, I was usually able to shake my shyness if I was given an opportunity to show off my athletic skills.

I sat attentively, crisscross applesauce, near the front of the huddle of kids. The gym smelled like Elmer's glue. I fidgeted with a stray staple that had landed on the floor while my teacher passed out flyers full of prizes that would be awarded to those who raised enough money. (Even as kids, we all knew the students with the richest relatives would win most of the prizes, but we let ourselves imagine, flipping through the prize catalog as if we had a chance.)

"We're also going to talk about heart health," my PE teacher continued. "Heart disease is the leading cause of death in the United States."

This is where the discussion began to go downhill. The words *leading cause of death* caught my attention. I was not prepared to die anytime soon, so I had to be aware of anything that might threaten my thriving young existence.

"Does anybody know the warning signs of a heart attack?"

Nobody raised a hand. We were a group of young public school kids who had little experience regarding medical matters. My teacher proceeded to rattle off symptoms: feeling light-headed, having chest pain, breaking into a cold sweat, gasping for breath.

I paused. The symptoms repeated themselves in my brain: *light-headed, chest pain, sweat.* As my teacher spoke, I noticed a sickening wave passing over my body. An alarming cool sweat crept into my palms. My head started to spin. My lungs forgot their purpose. The phrase *leading cause of death* rumbled around my skull. My brain was so new, and it was especially susceptible to bad habits. I let my thoughts cascade down a trail of what-if questions: *What if I die of a heart attack? What if I'm experiencing a tiny heart attack right now? What if thinking about heart attacks can actually give me a heart attack?*

The thoughts made my heart beat with heightened aggression. I swore I could feel a sharp pain stab through my shoulder and into my neck. It all felt so real. The realest thing in the whole world.

I had always been a sort of anxious kid. I couldn't fall asleep without a night-light. I still had a lot of trouble speaking in the presence of strangers. Sometimes, I convinced myself that twisting my earrings could ward off bad luck. But in class that day, my general nervousness gave way to true terror. Just like that, I thought I might be dying.

Part of me wanted to raise my hand and beg for help—or at least ask to be sent to the school nurse—but the other part of me knew I would raise a few eyebrows if I declared in front of the whole class that I was having a heart attack right after we'd spent fifteen minutes talking about heart attack symptoms. I wasn't dumb. I knew my fear was irrational, but I couldn't ignore the way my own flesh turned on me—the way it broke into a full-body sweat. I decided against asking to go to the nurse, and I resorted to the next-best strategy: asking to go to the bathroom. I figured that if I was going to die, at least I would save myself the embarrassment of dying publicly, under the scrutiny of my classmates.

When I got to the bathroom, I locked myself in the biggest stall and paced around its humble square. Luckily, nobody else had to pee. I was able to hyperventilate in peace. I tried to close my eyes and imagine I was at the beach—a technique my mom had taught me when I woke up with bad dreams—and it helped a little, but not much. I went back to pacing. My heart was beating so loudly, I could hear it. The thumping nearly echoed off the walls. I counted the tiles on the floor. When I lost track, I started over. I don't know when I started to cry, but at some point, I noticed that my cheeks were wet. It felt like the earth had split open, and I was the only person who noticed at all.

I'm not sure how much time passed, but eventually the thumping in my chest quieted. The sweat receded from my palms. I inhaled, and my lungs worked exactly as they were supposed to. I looked in the mirror. My face was inflamed, pink; I could see my distress even through the clouded mirror. I twisted my earrings a few times, and I wiped my eyes. I didn't want to, but I returned to class, sneaking into the back of the room, hoping nobody realized how long I had disappeared.

I never told anyone about the episode. I thought it would be a one-time thing, but I was wrong.

The tiny heart attacks didn't go away.

They kept showing up. A few days after the first incident, my brain started spiraling during a science lesson. I had been doodling in the margins of a worksheet when my thoughts wandered somewhere dark. The room was silent, and my brain filled the quiet up with worries. My thoughts all formed into dreaded what-ifs. *What if I start feeling like I'm going to have a heart attack again? What if I can never stop thinking about heart attacks? What if this time my heart really stops?*

Within seconds, the symptoms came back, and I was sure that I was dying. Maybe the first tiny heart attack had been a false alarm—but this one, this one had to be the real deal. I could *feel* it.

I left for the bathroom. I don't think I even bothered asking for permission. I locked myself away until I had counted every single tile on the floor.

Again, I told no one.

The tiny heart attacks started showing up more frequently after that. One arrived during silent reading time as the rest of the class looked down at their books. Another appeared while I was riding the bus to a field trip, and I stared out the window so nobody would notice the dread in my face.

I even managed to convince my parents to let me skip school the day that Jump Rope for Heart rolled around— I was too nervous to participate. I faked a stomach bug. I was sure the event would spur another tiny heart attack, so I didn't go.

Even in its earliest stages, my anxiety seemed to link itself to my body.

I was just a kid, but I stopped viewing my body as a thing I could trust. I knew that at any minute my inner gears could fizzle and give out. I suddenly understood, with unnerving clarity, that I would eventually die. It was a searing knowledge to gain vision of, and sometimes I could hardly see past it.

It would be years before I learned the term *panic attack*. The words should have come as a relief. They explained that my heart actually wasn't going to burst at any moment. But learning that the real threat was all in my head didn't necessarily make me feel better—mostly, it made me feel like I had an even bigger secret to hide.

This realization—the realization that my brain was to blame—somehow reached beyond my primal fear of death. Although I had believed that the tiny heart attacks might actually kill me, I was even more terrified of being seen as someone who had completely lost her mind.

3

Tongue-Tied

In the fourth grade, I nearly bit clean through my tongue. Even now, if I rub my teeth over the tip, I can still feel a tiny bump of a scar. I always find myself accidentally grazing it when I chew gum too mindlessly or when I speak too quickly.

It happened right after I turned ten. One spring morning, I woke up before dawn for skating practice. I was lost in thoughts of sparkling dresses and Olympic gold medals, believing my dreams were on the verge of coming true. At that point, I had been skating for nearly five years. I had progressed through the local rink's beginner classes, and I had begun to train more seriously with a coach before school. I even began traveling for competitions. In the fall and winter, my mom and I would road-trip to California together so I could compete against other young skaters in my region.

That particular morning, as I had hundreds of times before, I pulled the laces of my skates tight, bending into the supple leather to test the flex of the boot, and walked over to the ice. My favorite part of the day was skating those first few laps. I circled in relative darkness, before anyone else made it to the rink, listening to the hum of the compressors that kept the ice frozen. The sound of my skates reverberated off the metal bleachers, and I felt vast, expansive, whole.

Too soon, my coach arrived, followed by other skaters, and I was forced to find focus within my aimless freedom. She ordered a basic exercise that entailed skating from one end of the rink to the other while performing jumps of increasing difficulty on each pass. I breezed through the first few, but as I went to take off for a jump that I had performed countless times before, something went awry on the entry. Like water spilling from a glass, I tumbled without any sense of form. By the time I looked up—my body puddled against the ice—a group of other skaters had surrounded me.

"Are you okay?" they chanted, one after another.

I knew I was in trouble when I couldn't open my mouth to answer. I rushed off the ice and into the restroom to view the damage in the mirror. Somehow, during the dramatic descent, my teeth had punctured my tongue, leaving a little corner clinging to the rest by only a thread. I wondered why my mom didn't take me to the doctor to get stitches, but she assured me that I would be fine (she had consulted with my surgeon grandfather, who assured her that this type of wound heals fairly well on its own). She found me some ice cubes, and I sucked on them as we headed to school.

Oddly enough, class started off in one of the best ways it could have in elementary school: with snacks. My mom informed my teacher and the school nurse of the little accident that had occurred earlier, and the nurse sent me to class with a bunch of Otter Pops to help soothe my wound.

At that point in my school career, I wouldn't have called myself an outcast, but I wouldn't say I was the coolest kid in the class either. I was starting to realize that other kids were discontinuing the impressed expressions they used to offer when I managed to raise my hand with an answer to the teacher's question. Some girls rolled their eyes when I fought too hard during the PE soccer games. Boys didn't bother passing me notes in class. A teacher called me bossy once when I had been appointed the leader of a club and had tried to organize members into various tasks.

The day I bit my tongue, I was forced to keep extra quiet, and the low profile allowed me to go fairly unnoticed.

My teacher began class by explaining why I wouldn't be talking.

"Karina had an accident at the rink this morning, so she won't be able to answer questions. That's also why she gets to have the freezer pops—and no, you *cannot* have one too."

I tried to avert my eyes from the collective gaze of twenty-four little heads turning all at once to look at me—checking to see the damage. When there wasn't a horrific scene to satisfy their stares, they turned away to focus on the math lesson.

Long-division problems appeared on the whiteboard, and the teacher scanned the rows for a volunteer. I was frustrated that I was sidelined from the experience. I knew the answers and wanted to be part of the action, but without being able to speak aloud, all I could do was write down the numbers and let the boy next to me, Jake, peek over at my paper and raise his hand, claiming to have conquered the finer points of 144 divided by 6. Even though I hated his guts, I didn't make a fuss. How could I? When the teacher applauded his efforts, he whispered kindly to me, "Thanks."

Okay, I thought. *Maybe he isn't so bad.*

The class headed to the lunchroom. While my friends snacked on peanut butter and jellies and gossiped about Jake (he happened to be a boy with a laugh that caused his head to tilt back toward the sky . . . a laugh that made most of the girls crumble with crushes), I watched and picked at my off-brand pudding cup. I nodded here and there, expressing approval and disapproval at certain statements through slightly exaggerated facial expressions. The conversation turned to the earlier math lesson:

"Did you see how he knew all the answers today?!" one girl said, giggling.

"He's so smart!" another added.

I focused my energy on my pudding, stirring the plastic spoon back and forth but hardly taking a bite. These same friends of mine would roll their eyes when *I* was the one who knew the answers. I wished with all my ten-year-old fury to tell them that Jake only knew because I'd let him copy me, but when I opened my mouth, my tongue fumbled a little before I quickly retracted it, hoping my attempt to speak had gone unnoticed. I sighed, knowing that sharing my secret about Jake wouldn't make my friends like me any more anyway.

PE began, and I sat on the edge of the basketball court, watching kids play as I ate yet another Otter Pop. I was really eager to join the team—my feet tapped the sideline, itching to get up and play. But since I wasn't able to, the girls who usually sat on the sides because they "forgot their tennis shoes" came over and began talking to me. They all possessed the ability to not care in a way I never would.

Even as they approached me, I tried to contain my anxious please-be-friends-with-me heartbeat to seem less eager. I averted my attention from the basketball game and listened while they shared their opinions of various Nickelodeon TV shows. I hadn't ever seen any of the shows, but I liked that they were including me. I nodded, pretending to know what episode they were giggling about, and I smiled, feeling somewhat accepted.

At the end of the day, my mom picked me up from school. I hopped into the minivan, and she asked if my day had gotten better since the rough morning. I thought about the question. . . . It was *hard* staying quiet. There had been so many things I wanted to say, so many times I longed to participate. But it seemed as if people liked me better this way: more silent, less visible. Nobody made fun of me for answering questions. Nobody made faces because I said the wrong thing. Nobody called me bossy. I decided it had been a pretty good day. I looked my mom in the eyes and nodded.

The next couple of days, my tongue still hurt, but I found myself able to talk more and more without fumbling over words. My wound healed remarkably well. Even when all that was left of the injury was the scar, though, I kept feeling a sharp pain whenever I went to answer a question, whenever I laughed too loud, or whenever I cared in a way that I knew was uncool. I almost couldn't

4

An Education

At the eighty-second Academy Awards, Carey Mulligan arrived in a black ball gown. She was nominated for best actress for her role in the film *An Education*. She walked the red carpet sporting what might have been the most beautiful blond pixie cut this earth has ever seen.

I was thirteen years old. I'm sure I had seen other pixie cuts before, but none of the others stuck out in my mind. Until then, pixie cuts belonged to older women who were tired of laboring over their shoulder-length bobs—women who couldn't be bothered with the trouble of suburban beauty. Otherwise, short hair was for boys.

That night, I sat too close to the TV. I stared at the

screen for the entirety of the awards show, hoping the camera would pan back to Carey and her perfect hair. I picked at the edges of our couch pillows. I hadn't actually seen *An Education,* but I desperately rooted for the movie to win every award. During commercial breaks, I googled the trailer for the film on my older brother's laptop so I could see Carey in action. I was disappointed to discover that in most of the scenes her hair was long, brunette, and parted down the middle. She was still beautiful, but I wanted to see more of her at the Academy Awards, with her wispy white-gold bangs. I image-searched pictures of her at various red-carpet events. She looked so striking and simple, and so feminine, and so unexpected—and every time she appeared on the screen, I had to hold my breath to keep from whispering the words *My god.*

All at once, I learned that there was so much about being a woman that I had not yet explored.

I wasn't sure what it was about her that made me feel all that yearning. I didn't know if I wanted to look like her, or if I just wanted to be near her in case a gust of wind blew a couple of strands of her hair out of place. I thought about how I would tuck them behind her ear.

Carey didn't win the Oscar for best actress. The show ended, and I finished my homework so I could go to bed. My own dark brunette waves splayed across my pillowcase like the arms of a ragged octopus.

The next day, I stood at the mirror with my flat iron,

smoothing out my tresses until they hung all the way down to my chest with an unnatural stiffness and shine. I don't know why, but I didn't even consider cutting my own hair. Habits can be so hard to break.

Spoiler!

Nearly a decade later, I took Carey's picture into a hair salon. *Like this,* I told the stylist. *I've always wanted to look something like this.*

5

Eighth Grade in Three Stories

They say things happen in threes—good things, bad things, always in threes. Sometimes, on nights when I felt particularly anxious, I used to count to three over and over again in my head until I could fall asleep. *One, two, three. One, two, three.* (I tended to believe that the tripling of negative scenarios was more likely than the tripling of positive ones.) I counted to distract my brain from its fears.

When I was in eighth grade, three things happened that somehow all felt related, though it might not sound like they are: I had the worst skating competition of my entire life; I went to the school dance alone; I made my period stop showing up.

The first event came as a surprise. At fourteen, I had reached the height of my singles-skating career. Oftentimes, when my mom and I road-tripped up and down the West Coast for competitions, I returned home with medals clanking around my neck. When my skates were laced up, I wasn't shy. I felt like a champion. I could jump pretty high. I could spin fairly fast. I was just beginning to discover the power in my legs, and I tossed my limbs across the rink with more speed than ever before. Skating felt something akin to motorcycle riding or cliff diving without all the risk. It was breathtaking.

I was coming off a really good season. For several years, I had struggled with my jumps, unable to rotate enough in the air for easy landings, but I seemed to be finally getting the hang of things. I had managed to master my double jumps, and I was beginning to work on triples. Although my toughest competitors were nailing most of their triple jumps, I had still managed to squeak onto podiums at my spring and summer competitions. For what I lacked in natural ability, I made up for in charisma.

Everything seemed to be going in my favor when I showed up at the regional championships in October. The sun was out. My heart raced in a good way.

As I made the trek from the parking lot to the rink entrance, I pulled my shoulder blades back toward my spine and stacked my vertebrae atop one another in order to stand as tall as my petite frame allowed. I had prepared all year for this competition—I was sure it would be my best regionals yet.

The rink was a dingy warehouse-like building in the middle of Southern California that smelled of hockey players and swamp. But despite its cavernous appearance and assaulting scent, it had a kind of charm. The ice was smooth and clear. The air conditioner reverberated with anticipation. All the skaters crowded on benches next to the snack bar, and we stared into tiny mirrors to touch up our faces—painting lipstick over our braces, coloring our cheeks with rouge to conceal our sprawling acne bumps.

My warm-up went well. I hurled myself through a few jumping passes. My toe pick gently gripped the ice every time. I glided through perfect landing after perfect landing.

"There is one minute remaining in this warm-up, skaters," an announcer's voice boomed.

I always spent the last minute of my warm-ups the same way: I took one final lap around the rink. I inhaled with a deep, full-bodied yawn, and then I looked out toward the crowd. I savored the collage of their faces. I took in the fact that—for about three minutes—the audience would be watching only me.

"Skaters, your warm-up is over. Please exit the ice."

We all skated off—everyone except for a slight girl in a pink dress, who was first to go.

I tried not to watch my competitors, but I was tempted to look over from time to time. I couldn't help but notice the ways other skaters were stronger than me. The pink-dress girl had faster spins. I watched her take her bows, and then a yellow-dress girl took the ice. She proceeded to land jumps that I had never even tried.

I plugged headphones into my ears, and I attempted to take my mind somewhere else. I counted in my head to distract myself from my nervous thoughts. *One, two, three.* Most skaters dreaded skating first, but I always dreaded skating last. The wait was making my legs grow cold. I stood up to shake them awake. My laces suddenly felt like they had been pulled too tight. I sat down to untie and retie them again. I couldn't force my body into stillness. I hated the waiting. I had too much time to think and worry. With adrenaline in my system, my knees began to twitch. All the excitement I had felt earlier got sucked into a vacuum. I found myself wishing the whole competition was over with.

When the announcer called my name, his voice sounded garbled and distant. I couldn't bring myself to look back into the crowd. My coach gave me a parting hug, and I skated to my starting pose.

The initial notes of my selection from Tchaikovsky's

Romeo and Juliet echoed through the speakers. The sound was harsh and imposing. The rink's fluorescent lights seemed too bright.

The rest of the performance is a fog in my memory. I know that nearly every jump went up and then lost its axis somewhere along the way. My body promptly came down against the cold surface each time. I had fallen before, but I had never felt so disconnected from my limbs. The notes of my music kept playing, solemn and taunting. The jarring sounds reminded me that the score of *Romeo and Juliet* was meant to serve as background to a tragedy. I had to fight the urge to skate off the ice. I kept going through the motions of my program, but only barely. I stopped performing. I couldn't hide the disappointment on my face.

The event sent me into a tailspin of mourning that lasted weeks.

For several days, I couldn't get out of bed. I hardly bothered to eat. My mom tried to console me, humming, *It's just skating—you'll have other chances,* but the sound of my disappointment drowned her out.

When I tried to show up to practices again, I found myself bursting into heavy sobs. I hated publicly crying, but I couldn't stop. The more I tried to stifle my tears, the more severely they wedged in my throat.

I felt the stares of the other skaters. Ice-rink drama was nothing new. I had observed my own share of minor disasters; at the rink, tears erupted from a different teenage girl nearly every week. But I had convinced myself I wasn't like the rest of them.

While the other skaters fixed their eyes on me, I became acutely aware of the ways I had talked about their emotions. I suddenly remembered the things I had said when they had dissolved into sobs after practices or wept exaggerated tears near the boards of the rink. *She's so sensitive. She's so dramatic. She doesn't need to cause such a scene.* My own criticisms echoed back at me.

My coach—a thoughtful, breezy woman I adored—tried to soothe me.

"What's going on?" she asked, clearly confused. "Let's try to talk about it."

I wiped my tears on my jacket sleeve. "I hate that I feel so much," I said. "I just don't want to be the kind of girl who feels this much."

I tugged my hair into a ponytail with an unnerving harshness. I swallowed and tried to strangle any tears I had left. I didn't necessarily want to feel happy again, but I definitely wanted to stop crying—I would have settled for feeling nothing at all.

The eighth-grade dance was the first big dance of my public school career. By the start of the spring semester, the talk of every lunch-table clique centered on the question of who was going to the dance with whom.

Of course, some students had easy answers. There were the kids who were already coupled up. They asked one another with balloons and teddy bears and poster boards. It was like a second Valentine's Day. The rest of us watched on with hidden resentment. I struggled to understand why pairings came so easily to some girls. No boy had ever expressed the slightest interest in me.

Nevertheless, I had my heart set on a boy who sat next to me in math class. He was shy and smart, and he seemed to have an eternally sniffly nose, which I somehow found endearing. I think most of all I was hypnotized by his habit of constantly flipping his hair out of his eyes. I adored the way he tossed his neck sideways with a flick, only for his bangs to fall down again seconds later. At fourteen, this was my idea of romance: observing—from a very safe distance—the specific details and intricacies of another person's quirks.

The flippy-haired boy and I talked quite a bit during class, which was impressive, given the fact that I rarely spoke to anyone outside my small circle of friends. He sometimes complimented my elaborate homework doodles, and he poked fun at the way I tapped my pencil—*one two three, one two three.* I prayed that his teasing meant he was also crushing over me.

"So, are you going to the dance?" I asked him one day,

in a bold moment of reckless abandon. He flipped his hair out of his eyes.

"No, I don't think so. Dances aren't really my thing."

I took his answer to be a reasonably good sign—at least he wasn't planning on asking some other girl! As the days passed, I considered the prospect of asking him myself. Maybe he was too shy to make a move. Maybe he needed a girl (me!) to give him a nudge. I toyed with the idea in my mind. The worst he could say was no. I daydreamed about casually bringing up the possibility of our pairing in the coming days, but I ended up abandoning my plans because—shortly after my daydreaming began—an acquaintance arrived at my lunch table with an exaggerated gasp. She dropped her cafeteria tray, and she pressed her hands to the table in a theatrical gesture of disbelief.

"Did you all *hear* what happened at first lunch?" she breathed. My friends and I were always the last group to get ahold of school gossip. We relied on casual peers and friends of friends to keep us informed.

The acquaintance with the scoop detailed the situation at hand: A girl from our social studies class had asked one of the football players to the dance. Normally, this kind of event wouldn't have been particularly shocking, but the girl was known to be a bit of an outsider. She got good grades. She was visibly eager and earnestly Christian, and she wasn't the type of girl who typically dated football players. That was what made the news gossip-worthy.

Despite the barrier of our middle school pecking order, the girl from our social studies class had been bold enough to seek out a date for herself.

Apparently, the football player had been kind. He had rejected the girl with tact—told her that he was sorry, he was flattered, but he already had plans to ask someone else.

I couldn't get past the way my acquaintance relayed the news. Her voice carried a hint of *How dare she* while discussing the earnest girl's attempt at taking her own shot at romance. She spoke as if the eager, awkward girl had committed a crime.

My stomach rolled over. There was no way I could ask the flippy-haired boy. I had been wrong. Getting rejected wasn't the worst thing that could happen—not at all. The worst thing was this: I could be next. I could be made into another girl who dared to want more than she was given. I could be next week's lunch-table news.

I decided that attention and affection were both overrated. I didn't dare bring up the dance to the flippy-haired boy ever again, and I went to the dance alone.

The first time I made my period stop, I felt like a minor god. I felt a very small ripple of power—like I had finally gained the upper hand over my unpredictable, erratic body.

It happened near the end of the school year. The entirety of April passed by, and nothing showed up. No deep red stains against my pajama bottoms. No cramping in my lower back. No headaches that took me out for days.

I had started dieting. It didn't seem like a big deal—not at first. Everyone at the ice rink was on some kind of diet. *I'm not eating bread, I'm not eating dairy, I'm not eating meat*—the sentences could have belonged to any one of us. Some skaters swore that the diets made them jump higher and skate faster, but looking back, I doubt any of the claims were true. Some diets might have been spurred by coaches, but that wasn't the case for me. At fourteen, I was still gangly. Nobody had told me to lose weight (yet). I was naturally small—barely any hips or chest rolling from my edges yet. I already looked like everyone's assumptions about figure skaters: I was a princess-like waif of a girl.

It wasn't just skating, though. My friends at school had started dieting too.

At the beginning of eighth grade, we all bought our lunches from the cafeteria. We ordered pouches of french fries and split them among our table. The fries were sometimes traded for bites of cookies or pizza crusts. Grease lined the ridges of our fingertips. We didn't think about what we ate. We just ate.

But somewhere along the way—sometime between the essays and the science tests and the school assemblies—we learned how to eat more carefully. Maybe some of the girls picked up habits from their older sisters. Maybe some learned from their mothers. Maybe some—like me—found a hundred tips on the internet to *drop five pounds fast* or *get slim for the summer.*

Maybe I just started dieting because I had always been so shy, and dieting became an easy thing to talk about.

Regardless, I started bringing my lunch to school. My sweet dad packed me lunch anytime I asked and would follow my careful instructions. I wanted only wheat bread for my peanut butter and jellies. I would take carrot sticks instead of cookies. No, I didn't want chips, or Cheetos, or anything fried, please. He probably thought my faux health kick would just last a week or so. I honestly thought so at first too, but I found myself quickly surprised at how easily dieting came to me. I felt a rush. At lunch, I counted my bites. *One, two, three.* It felt good to be successful at a thing that people usually said was hard.

I knew that my lack of a period was probably a result of my shrunken meals. I had heard rumors from older girls at the rink. They mentioned that dieting could sometimes make a body halt its constant changing. To me, it seemed like dieting could make time stand still. Of course, restricting meals was not an actual means of acquiring eternal youth. My disappearing periods could be explained by the basics of biology. When a human body doesn't receive enough nutrients, its systems begin to shut down. I wasn't really halting time. I was just hurting myself.

One night, I looked at a full box of maxi pads in my bathroom cabinet and remembered my first period—the one that came right after my eleventh birthday. I had felt a secret pride in hitting puberty before the rest of my friends. I had relished the thought of getting to be a woman—a beautiful creature with a flowery scent and a curving chest.

I tucked the maxi pads away, into the cabinet's back corner. I knew I wouldn't be needing them—at least not for a while. I felt myself swell with secret pride once again, but this time, the pride was not in my body's ability to grow—it was in my body's ability to diminish. Becoming a woman was not what I had expected. My legs and arms and armpits had sprouted alarming dark hair that I was too embarrassed to ask how to shave away until my classmates began to notice. My skin had rippled with tender pimples. My eyes had given in to a desperate need for glasses. Womanhood was not transforming me in the ways I thought it would. A boy in the hallway called me manly once, and his words echoed through my own thoughts for the rest of the school year.

I didn't think of myself as a beautiful creature anymore, and it broke my heart. Starving felt like stealing the smallest piece of womanhood back.

At the rink, other girls asked me: *What have you been doing? What's your secret? I wish I had your self-control.*

⁓

By the time eighth grade ended, I had convinced myself not to need too much of anything. I had convinced myself that the easiest way to be a woman was to pretend I could go without emotions, attention, and even food. I could ignore my wants simply by counting over the noise of desire in my head. *One, two, three. One, two, three.*

Years later, as an adult, I took a trip to a NASA visitor center, and I sat in a big auditorium listening to a presentation about female astronauts. The woman leading the presentation talked about a rigorous test that all astronaut trainees had to go through: They were forced to float in a sensory-deprivation tank for as long as they could stand it. The test was supposed to mimic the isolated, claustrophobic feeling of floating alone in deep space. The male trainees generally couldn't last in the tank for more than an hour, but the women—the women seemed to be able to float forever. Some female participants stayed in the tank ten times longer than the men; they bobbed in the water, unbothered, while an entire workday passed. Some women floated until the people running the test had to tell them to stop.

There are various theories that seek to explain why

women can withstand the effects of sensory deprivation longer than men, but I have a theory of my own: Women are taught the art of ignoring their needs from a very young age.

I imagine that, as a teenager, I would have done well in sensory deprivation. Fourteen-year-old me would have thrived in a cool, soundless tank. I would've counted until the people running the test pulled my dripping body from the water. I would've proved that I could float on my own—requiring absolutely nothing—until someone turned the lights back on.

One, two, three. One, two, three.

6

The Time I Was Surrounded by Nearly Fifty Thongs

I tried out for the dance team my freshman year of high school. In those days, I was all ballet buns and posture. Alongside my skating training, I took dance classes several times a week; there I had learned to pirouette on pointe shoes and sashay to maraca beats in a jazz class.

The kind of dancing I was familiar with was not quite the same kind of cheerleading-style movement I would be performing at high school pep rallies, but I still managed to impress the coach enough during my audition to land a spot on the team. I was excited to learn something new and get involved in an activity at school. Beyond classes, skating took up most of my time, so I didn't participate in many clubs or groups. I thought being on the dance team would be a good way to make friends—and I secretly hoped that it would impress some boys in my classes.

The first day of practice, I had my first experience with a women's locker room.

Our particular locker room was small and a dull, dusty shade of pink that looked like it belonged on the walls of a nursing home. One side of the room was lined with old movie-starlet mirrors, and on the other was a door leading to an oversized bathroom stall. The floors were dirty from the shoes of a hundred students marching in and out during passing periods.

On the first day, we all slid into the room and lined up to change clothes. There was an unspoken hierarchy to the procedure. The pretty, confident seniors stood up front, close to the mirrors. Their friends, juniors and sophomores, surrounded them along the side walls, and I stood near the back corner with a couple of other younger, quieter members of the team.

I was uncomfortable in my body before I ever had to undress in front of those older, effortless girls—some of whom were close to being women (beautiful, polished, perfect women!). My discomfort grew exponentially when it was revealed that, underneath her clothes, every single other girl on the team was wearing a thong.

Every single other girl.

I became hyperaware of the fabric covering my hips.

I backed farther into the corner and imagined my body folding over and over while I bit my lip and stared at the floor. In hindsight, I realize that it wasn't my body or my underwear that would've drawn attention but all my visible discomfort.

The other girls reapplied ChapStick in the mirror. They made conversation while slowly stepping into their gym shorts.

I averted my eyes from potential stares, but I was sure everyone was looking at me. My body felt chubby and ugly and entirely plain.

There was a kind of isolated ache that came from being surrounded by beautiful people and believing I was not one of them. It was a feeling that would later follow me to competition locker rooms, and lonely college parties, and even a public beach, where I convinced myself that I was the only person on the planet who had thighs that dimpled like they had been sitting against the pebbled shore for too long.

A whole year passed, and every day, I dreaded entering the locker room. I dreaded my pronounced efforts to avoid staring at the other girls—as if they were high school Medusas, ready to turn me to stone. And I dreaded the thought of other girls looking back at me; I was sure they could all see how unbearably different I was.

But none of the other girls ever mentioned it.

Nobody ever said a word about my unremarkable

panties. Today, I'm not certain anyone else even noticed. But just *feeling* like an outsider was enough to leave me reeling. In my head, I convinced myself that other people were thinking the same horrible things I thought of myself.

I ended up quitting the dance team at the end of the year. It wasn't entirely because of the panties, but maybe in a small way it was. I guess I decided that it was easier to leave than it was to stay somewhere I thought I didn't belong.

Spoiler: When I eventually got my driver's license, one of the first things I did was drive to the nearest Target and carry a handful of thongs to the checkout counter. I couldn't bring myself to make eye contact with the cashier. I wasn't on a dance team anymore. I wasn't changing in any high school locker rooms. Nobody was going to be looking at my underwear for quite some time. I'm still not sure what I was trying to prove or who I was trying to prove it to.

Becoming a woman always seemed to feel that way— like scrambling to catch up, like never quite understanding what I was trying to catch up to.

7

The Tent Party

While I never managed to collect a lasting group of friends from the dance team, I did find myself a posse of girls from my AP classes. We clustered together like a school of fish in order to survive the lawless high school hallways. We were a bit nerdy, and a bit naive, and we almost all had parents or grandparents who were immigrants. We liked the same bands, and we watched the same artsy movies, and that was enough to bond us inseparably. For the most part, we were boyfriendless, and we shamelessly devoted our time to one another.

Among the countless nights we spent sleeping over and swapping secrets, there is one that remains vivid in our memories: the night of the event we have since dubbed the Tent Party. It took place when we were all about fifteen, sometime during the crease between fall and winter, when Arizona finally cools down enough for wearing sweaters and drinking beverages that aren't almost entirely composed of ice.

My friend Rayna came up with the idea to host an entire camping trip in the comfort of her backyard. We would pitch a tent, roast marshmallows, and tell ghost stories, but we would still have easy access to the modern conveniences of indoor plumbing, refrigerated foods, and, of course, Wi-Fi. (I still think this is the most brilliant way to go camping.)

By the time I arrived, the tent was pitched and a number of giggling shadows were already inside.

Somehow five teenage girls managed to squeeze into a shelter for two, but the lack of space didn't bother any of us. We huddled. Sodas and Gatorades found their way into every inch of space we had left over. A family-sized bag of candy corn sat at the center of us all. Cocooned in translucent yellow fabric and lit by a half dozen strategically placed flashlights, our bodies glowed in the ambiance of the whole scene. A haze like the inside of a cloud filled the space. Natalia—Nati, who was always the most rebellious one of our bunch—had brought a hookah pen and passed it around. Everyone took turns inhaling and puffing and making clumsy smoke rings—everyone except me, that is, because I was nervous, and because I have had asthma all my life, and struggling for air has given me a pretty strong aversion to inhaling anything besides oxygen. But my nervousness and my refusal to participate in even mildly illicit activities didn't matter—my friends let me gently pass the hookah along without any mockery or protest. I felt a sort of secondhand buzz from the closeness of our bodies as I waded in the fog of other people's breath.

We took turns googling Arizona ghost stories.

Did you hear the one about the lady who drowned her children in the pond? Did you hear the one about the girl who heard voices in the walls? Did you hear the one about the couple who drove by a farm one night and saw an animal sucking the blood from a cow?

Most of the stories were hybrid folktales—Hollywood-style horror mixed with Native American and Latin American myths.

After what couldn't have been more than ten minutes, someone said, "Let's do something else." I agreed without hesitation. We were all beginning to jump at the slightest chirp of crickets from outside the tent. Plus, I have never been a person who likes seeking out fear. I always have enough fear as it is.

"What if we play truth or dare?" Rayna suggested.

She was met with a chorus of nods. The idea seemed to be at least marginally safer than discussing various local hauntings. We started out with easy truths. We stole questions off the internet: *Who do you have a crush on? What was your most embarrassing moment? When was the last time you lied?*

Most of the answers we could have predicted with ease. We had forged a closeness from sharing secrets, and many of our confessions had already been spilled at lunch tables or passed as notes in quiet classrooms.

When we tired of truths, we moved on to dares. Those were easy at first too: *Chug a whole Gatorade without stopping for a breath. Lick a rock from outside the tent. Yell the word* penis *loud enough for the neighbors to hear.*

Then someone suggested a dare I wasn't prepared for—a dare that scared me even more than the ghost stories we had whispered in the dark. It wasn't even a dare made for me.

"Lindsay, bite on a candy corn and pass it to Mackenzie's mouth."

Nati was the one who suggested the dare.

Lindsay picked up a piece of candy corn and ceremoniously bit the edge. Candy corns are small—too small to pass one from mouth to mouth without brushing lips. So when Lindsay made eye contact with Mackenzie—the candy barely peeking out from between her teeth—both girls knew the feat would end in a kiss. They cautiously leaned closer until their faces were about to brush, and then they giggled and promptly pulled away. They tried again a few more times, but neither could commit to the dare. They blushed, and we moved on with the game.

I didn't necessarily have a crush on any of my friends, nor was there one specific friend I fantasized about falling for.

But I *was* curious.

And we *were* all so close. That night, I watched the boundaries of my female friendships blur in the slightest way. I felt myself hope for a similar dare, and I moderated my own disappointment when the game ended without my own chance at a kiss.

We eventually gave up on the camping experience. The tent's too-tight quarters kept us from getting comfortable, and we went back inside the house to sleep. I had forgotten to bring pajamas, so my friends let me borrow some of their extra clothes—a spare shirt from Rayna's drawer, an extra pair of track shorts from Nati's backpack.

The five us of all fell asleep in Rayna's bed, lined up like crayons.

That moment was the closest I had ever been to love: much closer than with the boys in class, who barely talked to me, much closer than the celebrity crushes I nurtured from afar. This was a mixed-up, still-discovering-itself kind of love, and even before I really knew what it was, I felt it weave through my rib cage.

I slept so soundly that night.

When I dig into the archives of my memory, my heart beats a little quicker as I think back to the hours inside the tent. I can recall the exact moment I silently wished for a dare under the flicker of the flashlights, and the haze of the secondhand hookah, and the sound of crickets chirping outside our tent.

I was sure women's lips would taste just like candy corn.

8

An Obsession

The summer after I turned fifteen, two ice-dance coaches started working at my rink. Until then, I had strictly been a singles skater.

Olympic figure skating is broken into four disciplines: ladies' singles, men's singles, pairs, and ice dance. Some key technical differences divide the disciplines. Singles skaters perform alone, executing a series of elements including jumps and spins. Pairs skaters perform as a two-person team, executing overhead lifts and throws. Ice dancers are a bit like pairs skaters—performing as couples—but they don't execute any jumps or overhead lifts. Instead, ice dancers focus on intricate patterns and precise step sequences.

Singles skaters are who most people picture when they think of figure skating. They're the ice princesses. The girls who often wear sparkly, short-skirted dresses. The ladies who land the triple axels . . . You probably know the type. And if singles skaters are the pop stars of the skating world, ice dancers are the underground-rock bands. They're less mainstream. They're edgier. For what they lack in fame, they make up for in aloofness and an alternative kind of allure.

Around the same time that the ice-dance coaches moved to my rink, I hit a lull in my singles career. My early Olympic dreams seemed to be fading. I wasn't landing many triple jumps, and I had to withdraw from the regional championships due to a torn muscle. The disappointment was beginning to make me lose interest in my sport—but if I'm being completely honest, I was enticed by the possibility of a different kind of life.

I had been watching my brothers flourish. They both played on the varsity soccer team, and they were constantly sun-kissed, surrounded by crowds of joking friends and crushing girls. I envied their social lives and their ability to balance athletics and fun. When classmates found out that my brothers and I were related, they all shook their heads in disbelief and exclaimed, *But you're just so different from them!* I felt alienated both from my peers and from my siblings, like I had been discovered as an imposter in my own family.

Meanwhile, as I spent endless hours at practices, I felt myself being forced away from the small, tight-knit group of friends I had managed to gather. While I went to ballet classes, Lindsay and Mackenzie went to the movies. When I attended physical therapy appointments, Rayna and Natalia hung out at coffee shops (occasionally meeting handfuls of dreamy, shaggy-haired guys who knew how to skateboard). I watched my dearest companions flirt with the prospect of expanding their lives and gaining boyfriends, and I floundered in an unnamed jealousy.

Plus, I knew skating was really expensive, and even when I managed to find time to venture along on my friends' escapades, I always felt too guilty to ask my parents for any extra spending money.

I thought about quitting all the time.

I was sure that I was missing out on the best moments of my fleeting adolescence for an impossible, frozen dream.

But then the ice-dance coaches arrived.

I had only a vague knowledge of their sport. I had seen ice dancing a few times on TV. I knew its competitions consisted of two programs: a rhythm dance and a free dance. The rhythm portion was a bit like ballroom dance, with rumbas and tangos and waltzes, and the free dance was wilder, with teams showing off all sorts of dance styles and techniques. I knew ice dancers skated with partners—but most important, I knew the discipline didn't require its athletes to land any jumps.

When the new coaches moved to my rink, I felt drawn to their side of skating. To say the least, I was intrigued by the prospect of skating without the tedious experience of tossing my body into the air. I started taking lessons with the new coaches for fun, but my slight curiosity quickly adapted into something more aggressive. It feels like an understatement to say that from the moment I began ice dancing, I fell in love.

Ice dancing *made sense* to me. Every step was choreographed. Every head turn and arm swing happened on a beat. Instead of big theatrical tricks, ice dancing centered on the details. The rhythms. The edges. Skating practices suddenly felt like I was tapping on piano keys. Like I was translating my body into language.

I began to excel in the sport. Where my Olympic dreams as a singles skater had begun to fade, my ambitions as an ice dancer were only just igniting.

My coaches encouraged me to register for the Solo Dance Series—a sequence of competitions for up-and-coming ice dancers who did not have partners yet—and I made my way through the ranks, winning almost all my events.

Suddenly my concerns about fitting in and missing out fell to the back burner.

"You have a lot of potential," one of the coaches told me. "If you can manage to find a partner, you'll be competing on the international circuit in no time."

That was all I needed to hear in order to develop a habit that teetered on the waterfall's edge of addiction. In my spare time, I watched old ice-dancing videos on You-Tube. I walled myself inside my bedroom, and I stared at my laptop until it left warm marks against my thighs. I became an encyclopedia of performances: I could recite the world medalists from any given year; I could list my favorite programs and my favorite teams and the most interesting elements from every competitive season since 1999. Sometimes, I even memorized exact sequences of choreography from the videos. I twizzled around my bedroom in my sock feet, mimicking the slide of the ice. I practiced turns and hair flips, and I tried to imagine what it might feel like to be lifted. When I finally fell asleep, I dreamed about tangos.

One night, I stumbled upon a video that would soon become my favorite. It was a performance by an Italian team, Anna and Luca. In the video, the woman wore a black-and-white-striped dress; her lips were painted red, and her facial expressions moved through the most captivating story. Her partner balanced at angles that seemed to challenge the existence of gravity. The couple skated to a piece of music from *La Strada*, an old black-and-white movie about lovers in a traveling circus. The skaters dipped and hopped to the music's whimsical notes. Trumpet sounds rumbled and bounced in perfect synchronization with their feet. The man lifted the woman, and she floated. Really floated. I held my breath for the entire four minutes of their program. While they skated, they built a world where little pockets of magic seemed to exist, and I wanted to live there—inside their steps and arm holds and spins. When the program ended, I swore I could smell the buttery notes of popcorn wafting in through my window. In the corner of my vision, I believed I could make out the glazed twinkle of carnival lights. I wanted, more than anything, to be whisked away to their circus. I decided that the best way to bring myself closer to their world was to transform into an ice dancer myself. When the performance was over, I hit replay, and I watched again, and I hit replay, and I watched again, and I hit replay . . .

During class the next day, I found myself counting waltz beats while my math teacher lectured on about y-intercepts and asymptotes.

One, two, three. One, two, three. Ice dance seemed to give even my strange, seemingly useless habits a purpose. Ice dance seemed to give every piece of me a reason to exist.

9

I Ruin Everything Fun

Although I was spending more and more time at skating practice, my friends were kind enough to keep inviting me to hang out. Mackenzie turned sixteen in May. She was the first in our group to get her driver's license. To celebrate the occasion, we packed ourselves into Mackenzie's car: a gold SUV that had been her mother's. She drove us cautiously to a nearby grocery store, where we planned to buy snacks and rent a Redbox movie.

We were still a relatively quiet bunch—rule followers, try-hards—but we were beginning to feel an urge to branch out. Maybe it was the freedom that our driver's licenses promised. Maybe it was just the natural gravity of teenage rebellion. Either way, the night glowed with potential.

We giggled around the grocery store. We danced through the aisles. We tossed the car keys back and forth between the five of us, and the mundanity of our little suburb seemed to turn on its head. Our cart overflowed: popcorn, pretzels, Cheetos, more beverages than we could possibly drink, box after box of sour candies that would later give us canker sores. I snuck glances at the nutrition labels while nobody was looking.

My body had changed—whether I welcomed the changes or not. My hips had become *hips*. My chest had turned into *breasts*. Even when I wasn't at the rink, I wore extra-tight sports bras because I hated seeing my body spill over itself. As I wandered the aisles with my friends, I made a mental note to keep track of how much I would later consume, so I could keep up with the calorie count that always tallied inside my head.

As we walked up to the register with rambunctious joy, the cashier glanced at us with a knowing half smile, and she didn't roll her eyes when we paid in cash, pooling together wrinkled ones and fives that had been smashed into the bottoms of our pockets.

When we squeezed back into the car, we reveled in the freedom of having a friend who could take us places. We no longer needed to rely on our parents for rides. We didn't have to bribe our older siblings with favors and birthday money anymore. It was an occasion that stirred our imaginations with a kind of nerve we had never felt before.

"We could really go anywhere," Rayna said.

"We could road-trip to California!" Natalia suggested, tossing her dark curls over her shoulder and smiling with her mouth wide open.

The daydream was tempting. California was an Arizona child's promised land. When we were younger, we all flocked to the state's southern beaches during spring break, and when we returned home, Arizona's sparkle always seemed a little bit dimmed. My friends and I grew up fantasizing about the coast and the suntanned people and the glamour of big-city stakes.

"We could get to L.A. by midnight if we left right now," Lindsay said.

I let out a nervous laugh. As much as I wanted to take an impulsive road trip, I couldn't get on board. We had finals in a few days. Where would we stay when we got to L.A.? What if our car broke down on the way? In a matter of seconds, I constructed nearly a dozen horrible what-if scenarios, all of which ended with me and my friends dying in the desert before we ever made it to the coast.

Luckily, Mackenzie intervened.

"I don't trust my driving skills to get us to California yet. I barely trust myself to take the freeway to Phoenix."

"That's okay," Natalia said without missing a beat. "Let's just drive around."

Lindsay plugged her phone into the aux cord and turned the speakers up until they shook under the weight of the bass. We sang along to cheesy boy-band pop music (we grew up in the golden era of One Direction), and we rolled down every window. Our voices cracked on the same high notes, and the wind messed up our hair. We felt incredibly unlonely, and it felt good.

Mackenzie gripped the steering wheel, trying to stay focused on her newly honed driving skills. She had been forced to take the driving test a few times (she was a good driver, but she always got nervous under the pressure of the DMV), and all those tests made her hyperaware of every road law in existence. She was cautious, maybe to a fault, but as we passed house after house—our windows down, the stereo up—she let her foot lean on the gas pedal a little heavier than she normally did. We cruised the streets of our neighborhood barely over the speed limit, and we watched the light posts and trees blend together in a watercolor blur.

I'm having fun, I thought. It was a habit I had picked up over time. I was so often being responsible and serious that I tried to call attention to the moments when I was actually enjoying myself. *This is fun,* I thought again, a bit surprised by my own joy.

We pulled up to a traffic light at one of the busiest intersections in our city. About a dozen lanes converged, and several lines of cars filed in like rows of dominoes. The cars all waited for their light to change so they could topple and continue on their way. Our light turned red just as we approached.

"Get out! Come on!" Mackenzie yelled, already unbuckling from the driver's seat. I heard the slam of a door and saw her dash past my window.

We all knew what she meant: that old prank where passengers run around the car until the light turns green again.

We followed her lead. We slammed our doors and sprinted, giggling the entire time. Eyes in the surrounding car windows looked on as we ran. Our arms overflowed with the grocery bags that precariously held the snacks we had just purchased. Our running quickly turned to dancing. We danced—full-bodied and reckless—in the middle of the road. Our pulses took over. The music from Mackenzie's stereo continued to play. I imagine the onlookers chuckled at us, remembering the silly joys of their own youth. Or maybe a few drivers rolled their eyes, annoyed by our childish antics. Either way, we didn't care. We kept dancing. For about a minute, we were able to shake up the monotony of our lives. For about a minute, we only knew delight.

Just when the light was about to change, I tripped, and

a water bottle toppled out of my bag and rolled into the center of the intersection. The traffic light turned green, and the car behind us honked. I didn't have time to retrieve what I had dropped. Instead, I stumbled back into my seat, abandoning the water bottle to its pavement grave, a relic of our careless prank.

Mackenzie drove us through the intersection. The rest of us rebuckled our seat belts and tried to make our lungs swallow short, eager breaths.

I looked out the rear window so I could see what had become of the bottle I had left behind, but there were already too many cars obstructing my view.

"I dropped a water bottled in the street," I said, concerned.

My friends just laughed, still dizzy from their elevated heart rates.

"Why didn't you just leave the grocery bags in the car? Were you planning on eating a snack before the light changed?" Mackenzie teased.

"I didn't have any time to think! I just got out of the car and ran," I said. I tried to speak jokingly, but my voice carried an unhinged pitch. I looked through the rear window again, wishing I could see what had become of the bottle.

My friends moved on. They went back to singing along to the boy-band music and feeling the wind in their hair. They watched the views outside their windows melt again.

I sat in the back seat, invisible, silent, disappointed—but unsurprised. I knew my joy could be extinguished so quickly.

A thought trickled from my brain to my body like a cool drop of rain. *What if a car swerves to avoid that water bottle and causes an accident?* That thought made the hairs on my arms rise all at once, and another horrible thought quickly followed: *What if my water bottle pops someone's tire?* Soon enough, the thoughts were a faucet. Then, minutes later, a flood. *What if somebody gets hurt because of my mistake? Oh god. What if someone dies?* I knew that each scenario was unlikely—but I also knew that *unlikely* didn't mean *impossible.*

My friends didn't seem to notice my body go stiff. They didn't seem to notice the way I'd gotten sucked into my own head so quickly that I was completely gone by the time we arrived at the next traffic light.

I knew better than to listen to my spiraling thoughts. I tried to reason with myself: *Nobody will swerve. Maybe after we drove away, the water bottle rolled out of the street entirely. Maybe a heavy truck passed through the intersection and crushed my stupid piece of litter.* My brain fought back against its own logic, asking again: *But what if someone dies? What if? What if?*

To my surprise, my friends confronted me when we arrived back at Mackenzie's house.

"You're being really quiet. Are you okay?" Lindsay asked.

"I'm fine. Just tired," I said. Since childhood, I had learned that tired could serve as a good excuse to explain the way I retreated into myself. It was easier to say I was tired than to try to describe the way my heart played vicious pinball games inside my rib cage. *Tired* was the next-best thing when I couldn't run away to a bathroom. Usually, nobody batted an eyelash at *tired*.

"No," Rayna insisted. "Something is wrong. You haven't been yourself for the last twenty minutes."

She was right, of course, but I wasn't accustomed to being called out. Usually, I was able to wallow in my mind, undetected. Over the years, I had fashioned myself into a decent actress. I had a dozen tricks for diverting attention away from my sweating palms, but I didn't have any practice with putting my panic into words. When I tried to find the language to explain what was happening—I couldn't.

"I'm just . . . ," I started out loud, and then I paused. I finished the thought in my own head: *I'm just crazy.*

My friends looked on with waiting stares. I sighed.

"I'm just really worried," I said.

"Worried about what?" Nati asked. She tossed her hair back. I was jealous of her. She often seemed so carefree and worriless (in the years I spent hiding my anxiety, I never really considered the possibility that other people might be hiding their own terrors as well).

"I can't stop thinking about the water bottle . . . how I just left it in the road," I said.

My friends' expressions didn't change. Their eyes searched for more of an explanation.

"What if it causes an accident?" I asked. "What if someone dies?" I added, more frantically. My voice came out strange—like someone was playing the harp with my vocal cords. As I pulled the sentences from my throat, I felt even more ridiculous. *I'm definitely crazy,* I thought. *I'm crazy, and now all my friends are going to think I'm crazy too.*

They just nodded. They didn't seem fazed.

"It's probably fine. I don't think anyone is going to die," Rayna said.

"Plus, nobody will know it was your water bottle," Mackenzie added. "The cops will never be able to catch you!"

I knew she was joking, and normally I would have played along, but I wasn't in the right mindset to bother with faking a laugh.

"That's not the point," I said. "I'll feel guilty for the rest of my life."

"Just try to forget about it," Lindsay said. "Let's turn on the movie. It'll distract you."

The movie was a comedy—full of men who elbowed one another at the punch lines of their jokes and women who made crude comments about sex that our parents wouldn't have approved of. My friends and I sat shoulder to shoulder on Mackenzie's couch. We opened several bags of popcorn and chips, but I hardly ate. My nervousness made my stomach churn, and I didn't feel like adding calories to the list of my worries.

My friends laughed along at all the right scenes. I made an effort to force a smile here and there.

"It's going to be okay," they each took turns reassuring me.

I tried to listen.

The next day at school, I continued to worry. It was unusual for my mind to spiral for so long, but I hadn't eaten or slept much, and the exhaustion kept me on edge. I could barely pay attention during my morning classes. I hid my phone under my desk and googled local traffic reports as my Spanish teacher conjugated verbs at the front of the room. Luckily, my teacher didn't seem to notice or care about my distracted behavior—or at least he was sympathetic enough to let it slide—and I continued to refresh the traffic report on my phone over and over for a full hour. There were no crashes listed at the infamous intersection, but that information didn't calm me. *What if the water bottle is still there? What if a crash just hasn't happened yet?*

I met my friends for lunch at our usual table—a booth tucked away at the side of the cafeteria. Rayna was already there, biting on a slice of pizza. Natalia was snacking while copying a page of Mackenzie's chemistry homework.

"You're still upset about the water bottle, aren't you?" Rayna asked.

She could see it all over my face—the worry and the shame. I wished I could just let things go, like a normal person.

"Look." Rayna gestured to a picture she had taken on her phone. It was the intersection. There was no water bottle in sight. "My mom drove us past the intersection this morning on the way to school. I made sure to check if the water bottle was still there. It wasn't. You can see for yourself. You can breathe now." She beamed at her own proof.

I sighed.

"Thank you," I said. "That makes me feel better."

I meant it. I did feel better, but for some reason, I couldn't stop tears from pooling above my lower lashes.

"I hate that I ruined last night," I said. "I hate that I ruin everything fun."

"You didn't ruin last night," Natalia said, still copying off Mackenzie's homework.

"Yeah, we all still had fun," Lindsay said. "It's okay."

And I could tell they weren't lying. And it was as simple as that.

My secret—my dark, hidden panic—was out in the open, and nobody seemed to mind at all. We went back to talking about movies and homework and whatever else was sparking our interest that day. I smiled and pressed my thumbs to the tops of my cheeks to stop the tears. Within a few minutes, I was already laughing again; my relief was so powerful, I felt giddy.

I'd spent my entire childhood operating as if my thoughts were a corpse I had to bury. Until the water-bottle fiasco, I had done a pretty good job of convincing myself that I could keep my panic under wraps, but after that night, I realized my friends probably knew about my anxiety all along. There was no hiding it from them, and there was no point—they loved me anyway. Even when I thought I was crazy, even when I couldn't control my horrible thoughts, they kept inviting me to their birthday parties, and they kept taking me on drives in their cars, and even when I was sure that doom was just around the corner, they would tell me over and over that things were going to be fine, and even if everything in my body told me otherwise, they made me want to believe them.

10

Mostly, I Wanted a Snow Day

I rode shotgun while my mom drove me home from an evening skating practice. Cars dotted the expanse of freeway in glossy red-taillight rows. The view through the front windshield could almost have been mistaken for the view of a lake—a wobbling reflection, all spots of light and color. We were stuck in rush-hour traffic. I took a deep breath.

"If I found an ice-dancing partner, would you let me move away to skate with him?" I asked.

I had been holding the wish inside myself—balled in a fist stuffed in a pocket. Although a small ice-dance community was growing in Arizona, the state wasn't exactly a hub for elite competitors yet. I knew that if I wanted to take my athletic career to the next level, I would need to start training alongside other high-level skaters and world-renowned coaches. I dreamed of moving to Colorado Springs or Detroit or Montreal—places where some of my favorite skaters trained.

When I spoke the question out loud to my mom, I sounded casual, as if this was the first time the thought had occurred to me, but my facial expression would have given away how invested I was in her answer. Luckily, my mom kept her eyes on the road.

"I guess so. If that's something you really want," she replied.

"Really?" I asked. I was surprised by her quick agreement. I had prepared a list of persuasive arguments in case she offered up a more hesitant response.

"Yeah. If that's your dream, I can't really say no."

"Cool." I paused. "Thanks."

With my elbow propped against my window, I leaned my head into my hand and smiled at the road ahead of me. My mom had always been the kind of person who kept her promises. She had watched my ice-dance obsession grow, and she had quietly nurtured my interest. She worked as a first-grade teacher, but whenever she wasn't in her classroom, she was driving me to practices and drawing designs for my skating dresses. It was obvious that my mom wanted to give me the world. But underneath her easy answer, she probably didn't think there was any real chance that I would find a partner. Partnerless boys are hard to come by in a sport overflowing with girls. Not to mention the fact that—at nearly sixteen—I was considered a bit too old to be starting a serious career. When my mom agreed with such ease, she likely wasn't anticipating a world in which my proposal was anything beyond hypothetical.

"In a couple of months, I'm going to remind you that you already said yes," I said.

My mom laughed.

A few months later, I managed to pull off my first big accomplishment as an ice dancer: I won my event at the National Solo Dance Final.

Skaters from all over the country had traveled to the competition, and as I stepped onto the top spot of the podium, I felt a sense of confirmation. I was *meant* for ice dancing. My hard work was paying off. I could picture my career filling with bigger competitions . . . maybe even international events!

But first I had to find a boy.

Winning the solo championships didn't guarantee that I would gain a partner. The accomplishment would boost my résumé, but the stars still had to align in order for me to find someone to skate with. . . .

The partner-matching process for ice dancers is a bit like dating. Everyone has certain qualities they're looking for. In order for a match to work, partners need to have personalities that complement one another. They need to have the same goals. They need to have compatible heights so that they can perform certain acrobatic feats. And because skating is still a sport tangled up in gender binaries, partnerships must be composed of one woman and one man.

Luckily for me, someone who seemed to meet all the right qualifications had been in the audience the night I skated at the National Solo Dance Championships. His name was Jonathan. He was an energized, flighty boy, and we happened to be training at the same level. He was relatively short, so he was looking for a girl who was pretty small. Standing just over five feet, I seemed to be an ideal match for him.

When the competition ended, his coaches contacted mine, and we arranged a tryout.

After a few weeks of organizing, I took a flight to meet Jonathan. It was a morning in late fall—so early that the moon could still be seen hanging around the sky.

My mom and I arrived at a small arena on the Colorado College campus. Outside the rink, a few students wandered toward a coffee shop. Inside the rink, the ice was soft and grayish. As I put on my skates, Jonathan bounced over to say hello. We quickly introduced ourselves, and then we took to the ice.

We spent a few hours waltzing with one another. I was surprised at how ordinary it felt to move with a partner, how easily my body hollowed into the contours of someone's arms. I intrinsically knew the mechanics of shaping myself to accommodate the presence of another person. I was like liquid—ready to adapt my own form to fit the outline of another's.

The tryout went well, and I was left with an opportunity: I could run away to Colorado Springs. I could start a new life as an ice dancer.

Remember. Remember when you said I could leave, I whispered to my mom on the plane ride home.

Neither of my parents could afford to quit their jobs and move to Colorado with me. I would have to go on my own. I would have to live with a host family and enroll in a new school. There were a thousand reasons for my parents not to let me go, but they let me leave anyway.

They knew that some chances only come once in a lifetime.

While a lot of suburban parents might have been nervous about sending their teenage daughter to live in another state, my mom and dad were surprisingly calm about the entire situation. This might have had something to do with the fact that my parents both lived far away from their own families at a young age—they met at an international boarding school when they were about thirteen—so when I asked to move across state lines for a shot at becoming an Olympic figure skater (and when my younger brother asked the next year to travel to Uruguay to train with the youth national soccer team), my parents couldn't help but support our lofty, adventurous goals.

Before I left for Colorado, my parents made me promise to stay home when the roads were icy, but otherwise they didn't try to stop me from slipping into a new life; they gave me permission to run away.

I finished out the fall semester of school, and then I spent my winter break sorting the entirety of my personal history into trash bags and suitcases and duffels.

The night before I left, I met my friends at a local frozen yogurt shop and said tearful goodbyes over spoonfuls of tart cherry. We promised to write each other old-fashioned letters, as if we were wives sending our husbands off to war. When the yogurt shop closed, we shuffled into Mackenzie's car just to sit in the parking lot. We spent the rest of the night passing around one of our phones and taking turns playing songs that made us relive good memories. We cried and cried into one another's arms. When we were together, our emotional upheaval didn't feel over the top. *These are the only people in the world who under-stand me,* I thought. I knew it was such a teenagerish thing to think, but that didn't make the feeling untrue.

The next morning, I woke up early. My dad's Honda Civic nearly overflowed with luggage. There was hardly enough room for my body to fit into the back seat beside the mess of disorderly belongings. The chaos was mostly my fault—I had done a terrible job of packing.

My brothers rolled out of bed to send me off. Luis had bought me a teddy bear. Marques joked that this wouldn't be a "real goodbye" because he didn't think I would last more than two weeks on my own. I assured him that I would survive at least three weeks—I could tough out almost anything if it meant proving him wrong. (For the record, I won the challenge; I ended up living in Colorado for over six years.) My siblings and I had never been particularly affectionate with one another. We were raised to show love in the form of practical jokes and borderline-cruel teasing, but in a rare moment of tenderness, I hugged both boys before I left, and I told them I would miss them. The sentimentality was unexpected, and before I could stop myself, I felt an invasive desire to unpack my bags. I didn't have time to question if I was making the right decision, though.

Instead, I hurried into the car. To keep from second-guessing myself, I focused on memorizing the exact color of my house as we pulled out of the driveway. I thought of words that might fit the shade: *flamingo-feather beige, dust-storm latte, warm-weather gray.*

We turned the corner out of my cul-de-sac, and my childhood slid into the past tense. My former life became a series of descriptions.

If I was being completely honest with myself, I could admit that the move wasn't one hundred percent about my dreams of becoming an Olympic ice dancer. Like most Chandler-raised sixteen-year-olds, I often fantasized about starting over somewhere new. During my freshman and sophomore years of high school (while my singles-skating career was hitting a shaky patch), I imagined quitting skating when I graduated and went off to college. I lusted after scholarships to prestigious schools on the East Coast. I threw myself into my grades, thinking they were my ticket to somewhere interesting and important . . . or at least someplace where it snowed every winter.

Then ice dance came along and gave me a chance to live somewhere snowy *before* graduation.

I saw the move as an opportunity for glorious reinvention: I would start wearing outfits I wasn't bold enough to wear in Arizona. I would learn to talk about obscure European artists and musicians. I would seem a little mysterious and a little aloof, and I would always leave my T-shirts half tucked. I would finally learn to speak fluent Spanish and maybe even French too. Other girls would turn their heads to stare when I walked through hallways. I would stop caring so much about everything. I would have a wry, unwavering look and personality and online presence. I would get invited to parties with ironic themes and crowds of strangers. I would get a grip on my emotions, and I would hardly ever sob. And I would stay thin—an elegant, seemingly effortless kind of thin. I would visit my hometown for the holidays, and people wouldn't even be able to recognize me.

I had these vivid, indulgent fantasies of becoming a new person, but for a long time, I thought I had to wait until college to put them into action. I was too afraid to test out a new version of myself with the same people I had known my whole life. When I got the chance to get away from the desert a little earlier than expected, I took it without a second thought. Colorado Springs wasn't New York City by any means, but it was still a place where nobody knew me, and it still promised the potential of an elusive, magical snow day, so I decided it would be good enough.

My parents reached out to circles of skating parents to help find a host family for me to stay with. This practice was relatively common in the skating community. There are only a few elite training hubs in the world, and skaters from all over are known to travel to be a part of them. After some research, we found the family of a pairs skater named Britney, a girl exactly my age, with a spare room in their town house. It seemed like the perfect fit.

For the most part, the trip to Colorado passed by quickly. My dad drove, holding hands with my mom while she periodically flipped through various radio stations. I wove in and out of sleep while nestled in the back seat. We made our way across the red landscape of my home state. I stared out the window, counting cacti and admiring them before they disappeared from my view. We crossed the border into New Mexico after about four or five hours.

The sun made its way down to the horizon just as we were approaching the southern edge of Colorado. I stared out the window and saw a sky full of tickled stars. The night was so clear, I felt like I was watching all the constellations gather for a party. Cassiopeia danced with Orion. The Gemini twins took turns cracking jokes. My world seemed bigger and grander than it ever had before. I could almost feel myself shedding the old version of me into a story.

I didn't even notice when the clouds rolled in.

In a matter of seconds, the view fogged over into a sheet of pristine white. I looked through the windshield; I could barely make out the glow of our Honda's headlights. My dad had let go of my mom's hand to grip the steering wheel with both of his fists. In turn, my mom gripped the armrest, as if it would help stabilize our tires while the road turned to ice.

A blizzard had erupted around us. The nearest town was still miles away. The road had all but disappeared. My dad was driving without any sense of sight. Occasionally, we felt the jarring bump of the rumble strips that marked the edge of our lane, indicating a need to alter our course. Just when we thought the weather would die down, a new gust of flurrying ice would obstruct our vision again. My mom silently prayed. I closed my eyes. It was easier to cope with the loss of visibility that way.

I thought about those stories on the news—the ones where people crash their cars during snowstorms and resort to extreme survival tactics to avoid freezing to death. My parents and I were not the survivalist type. We didn't have any outdoorsy skills. I still didn't even own a winter coat. . . .

I had asked the universe for snow, and it had been given to me. All of it, all at once.

After driving for almost half an hour without a town in sight, road signs for an upcoming rest area began to appear. By the grace of a generous god, our car made it to the small town of Raton, right on the cusp of the New Mexico–Colorado border. We spent the night in a motel that was nearly overrun with blizzard-weary travelers who had been forced to halt their journeys for the night. When I woke up in the morning, a blanket of powder still covered the parking lot, but the sun was shining again.

I had never experienced the quiet of a morning after a snowfall before. The flakes cushioned every sound. The world turned a little slower. When I stepped outdoors—still a little light-headed from the night before—I came to terms with the fact that starting over in a new city might not work out exactly as I planned. I should have known from all the time I had spent in ice rinks, but the snow felt so much colder than I had expected.

My parents and I continued the drive to Colorado. The rest of the trip was uneventful. Early in the afternoon, we pulled up to the town house that would be my new home. I told myself the hardest part was over: I had made it out. Despite a storm, despite the occasional impulse to tell my parents to turn the car around, I had arrived. I was starting over. I could be whoever I wanted now.

I walked up to the town house and knocked on the door. A perky brunette girl answered. She smiled, showing her teeth.

"I'm Britney," she said. "These are my parents, Sally and Di."

Standing behind Britney were her two moms—the first lesbians I ever (knowingly) met. I had met several gay men before: a handful of skating coaches at my local rink, a pair of boys at my high school. But until that moment, I had hardly considered the existence of gay women. Perhaps the moment should have illuminated something in the back of my mind. Maybe I should have noticed a flicker of recognition in my bones—but I didn't. I was too nervous about the move and too caught up in my crushes on boys to pause and truly think about the glorious reality of meeting two women who were in love.

When I tried to introduce myself, I felt my same old shyness pulling the words that I wanted to say back into my stomach, and I felt a new kind of nervousness that I couldn't quite place.

I looked back out the door and saw my new front yard covered in a bed of untouched flakes. The emptiness reminded me so much of an ice rink. It reminded me so much of a blank page.

11

So Much for Reinvention

The first couple of weeks in Colorado were hard.

Practices were exciting—I got to try lifts for the first time, and I liked the added speed that came from skating with another person—but I always got nervous when practices ended and I had to return home. Living with strangers was more challenging than I expected.

I should have become fast friends with Britney. We had so much in common: We both liked watching *Say Yes to the Dress* and baking banana bread and rolling our eyes at the stuffiness of the figure-skating world. But between my shyness and Britney's politeness, we struggled to form a friendship. I was scared of making small talk; Britney was scared of pestering me. We were like considerate ghosts with each other, only bothering to haunt ourselves.

Britney's skating partner, an older boy named Matt, lived in our basement. Matt was in his early twenties. He was outgoing and bold, and he wasn't particularly interested in the lives of two bookish sixteen-year-old girls, so he mostly kept to himself. During the day he trained at the rink with Britney, and at night he worked long hours at a seafood restaurant.

The three of us moved around our town house like carousel animals—somehow sharing the same space while always maintaining a safe distance from one another.

Sally and Di came to check on us all during the weekends. They both worked as teachers in Denver, so they spent their weekdays at another house, closer to their jobs. When my parents agreed to let me stay with a host family, I think they probably assumed the adults would be around more often, but I didn't want them to worry, so I didn't talk about how often Britney and I looked after ourselves. Besides, as uneasy as I felt around Britney and Matt, I felt an even greater skittishness in the presence of Sally and Di. They were unbelievably kind, but I still couldn't stifle the nerves that bubbled in my belly whenever they were around.

On weekdays, Matt, Britney, and I split the chores, rinsing dishes and folding laundry. For the most part, our days were surprisingly tame. Living in a house without the immediate presence of any parents sounds like an adventure, but in reality, it mostly just meant that I had to balance more responsibilities. I often thought about the teenagers in fantasy novels and how they always managed to take care of themselves while simultaneously saving the world, but in my life, functioning without many adults around wasn't so easy. Most days, I was just proud of myself if I managed to get all my homework done and make a dinner that had not been cooked entirely in the microwave.

I was relieved one afternoon when Britney announced she would be spending the weekend at her parents' house in Denver. It meant that I would be able to let my guard down. For a couple of days, I would have three fewer people to avoid while I tiptoed around the house.

Britney left on a Friday evening.

As soon as I heard the garage door close, I hurried downstairs to the kitchen. I made myself microwave popcorn, and I sang out loud while waiting for the timer to beep. I twirled half-heartedly, relaxing back into my body. I was surprised at how much I had grown to appreciate solitude. I actually felt lonelier around my housemates—their presence reminded me of the fact that nobody in Colorado truly knew me yet.

When my popcorn was ready, I scurried back upstairs. I took refuge in my bedroom, swapping my contact lenses for glasses and changing into an old set of pajamas. I tried to transform into my most comfortable self. Then I video-called my friends from back home. Their pixelated faces instantly warmed my skin. When I heard their voices say hello, I could almost imagine I was home again. Almost.

My friends and I talked for hours. They chatted about homework and the SATs and gossip and boys. I chatted about my new school: how everyone drove expensive cars and wore polo shirts . . . how the campus looked like it belonged in a teen movie . . . how I felt even more alone than I had back home . . . how I wanted people to call me by my whole name—Ana Karina—but hardly anyone bothered to learn my name at all . . . how, in history class, I couldn't find anyone to be my partner for a group project, and while I sat at my desk, I felt like I was falling into an abyss.

Nati bounced in and out of our video chat. Mackenzie's laugh bellowed, low and full, through my speakers. Rayna always had something smart to say. The girls looked like lifeboats. They distracted me with their own lives and reminded me that this was all part of a bigger adventure. They joked that at least I knew I wouldn't be the kind of person who peaked in high school, and their words made me feel a little better. As we were chatting, I heard a crash from the lower level of the town house.

"What was that?" my friends asked.

"It's just my roommate Matt," I said. "I think he's

watching TV downstairs. He must have the volume turned up really high. . . ."

We went back to talking. A few other noises rippled from below me, and I assumed they were the booms and clangs of an action movie. I ignored the sounds—I didn't want the world outside our call to exist.

Eventually, my stomach rumbled, and I felt compelled to grab some more snacks from the kitchen.

"I'll be right back," I said. As I made my way downstairs, I realized something was wrong.

The living room had erupted.

Matt had *not* been watching an action movie. He had thrown a party.

A few guests clutched bottles—champagne, tequila, rum—a half dozen shades of liquid gold. Girls danced on the furniture. They wore crop tops and heels. Boys made out with other boys on the couch. They gripped one another's muscled arms. I looked on, captivated for a few breaths. When I realized I must have been staring, I promptly turned away. The deep hum of pop music vibrated against the walls. The living room was messy in a seductive way. Jackets had been flung onto the backs of chairs; empty cups had been abandoned on the coffee table. Every mouth hung slightly ajar. Every face beamed with an alcohol-induced spark. The scene looked like a coral reef at night. It was beautiful—the colors, the chaos.

And I was there. In the middle of it all.

Except I hadn't been invited. And I'd shown up in my pajamas and glasses and a messy bun that wasn't messy in a cute way at all. And I looked entirely out of place.

As I waded into the kitchen, Matt spotted me.

"Oh, hey, Karina!" He sounded surprised—like he hadn't even realized I was home.

"Hey," I murmured back. "I'm just grabbing some snacks," I explained.

I dug through the pantry and darted back upstairs before Matt could say anything else. When I returned to my room, I threw myself onto the bed. I looked at my friends, who had been waiting on the other side of my laptop screen.

"You guys won't *believe* this," I began. "The party of the century has been going on in our living room all this time. I thought Matt had just been watching a movie. . . ."

"Get dressed! Go downstairs and crash it!" they encouraged me. "This is the moment you've been waiting for!"

The thought was tempting. Wasn't this what I had wanted—something new and adventurous? A night that could change me? Wasn't this what I had imagined when I'd decided to leave home and live among other teenagers?

I hesitated.

"No . . . I don't know anybody down there. I'll seem so misplaced," I said. "Maybe another time."

As I made my decision, I remembered the feeling of

sitting alone in history class, tracing the wood patterns of my desk and knowing that nobody was going to pick me to be a part of their group. I stayed in my room and felt the pull of a familiar abyss.

～

As weeks passed by at the rink, Jonathan and I geared up for our first competition together. We would debut our programs at a summer event in Maryland. When the trip neared, my competitive side reared its head. For me, it wasn't enough just to have a partner and attend the competitions. . . . I wanted to win. I wanted to continue to stand on top of podiums, even if it meant that I would have to work twice as hard as all my competitors. I had gotten a late start as an ice dancer, but I wanted to make up for lost time. I wanted to prove to myself that I'd left home for a good reason.

Between breaks in my practices, I observed my training mates.

Colorado Springs was home to some of the top skaters in the world. Most days, the rinks were occupied by international athletes, and even by Olympians, and whenever I stepped onto the ice, I hoped their success would rub off on me. I picked up their habits. I copied their warm-up routines and their cooldown routines and the outfits they wore to train in.

My every move was dictated by my desire to get an edge.

I arrived at the rink one day and found a group of skaters mingling in the lobby. They all wore the red-white-and-blue jackets that could only be earned by being named to Team USA. I recognized most of the skaters from various international events. There was a singles skater with dark eyes, and two pairs girls with matching bouncy ponytails.

While I signed up for my practice sessions at the front desk, I overheard the skaters talking. I shouldn't have been eavesdropping, but I couldn't help myself. Although the girls were around my age, I looked up to them. I wanted to be their friend—but even more than that, I wanted to live their same lives. I was willing to do *anything* it would take to work my way into their circle, to wear the same red-white-and-blue jackets they all wore. . . .

I quickly realized the girls were talking about their bodies. They were sharing diet tips and lamenting the way their legs *put on muscle too easily.*

And suddenly it seemed like the rinks in Colorado Springs were not so different from the rinks back home after all.

"I'm trying this new thing," the dark-eyed singles skater began. "On Sundays, I'm only drinking smoothies. No solid foods. I've been doing it for the last two weeks, and I feel like I'm noticing a difference."

The pairs girls nodded. Their ponytails sprang in agreement.

I thought: *Maybe next Sunday, I will try not to eat any solid foods.*

Spoiler alert. When Jonathan and I competed in Maryland, we scored somewhere near the very bottom. The top teams had years of experience under their belts that Jonathan and I simply couldn't contend with yet. Maybe I should have anticipated the results, but I was still disappointed.

I just need to be doing more, I thought.

I added different exercises to my workout routines. I improved my flexibility. I watched so many videos of tangos. I ate a little less.

12

Life Imitates Art

I ripped apart a peanut butter and jelly sandwich with my hands, accidentally rubbing a spot of charcoal onto the bread's spongy surface. I ate the entire sandwich anyway. I imagined the black dust tracing a line down my intestines. I briefly wondered what the calorie count of charcoal might be.

Several weeks had passed since my arrival at Cheyenne Mountain High School. In all that time (and despite my best efforts), I hadn't managed to make any friends, so I usually ate lunch in the art studio, where I couldn't be gawked at while sitting alone.

The studio was an airy, sunlit room with windows that opened up to the mountains outside. Art supplies were packed tightly in buckets and on shelves. Gigantic wooden tables were scattered throughout the room. At the table where I usually sat, some long-forgotten students had gracefully carved their initials into the wood.

I had taken up art classes my sophomore year, but I had nurtured a quiet love of drawing since I was a kid. Sketching reminded me of dancing: It was a very physical process. I stood up while I worked. I paced. Every time I reached for the canvas, I put on some sort of chaotic show.

The shudder of a door handle jolted me alert while I chewed the last bite of my sandwich. I tried to swallow before whoever it was could step all the way into the room—we weren't *technically* supposed to eat in the studio, but during lunch, the teacher wasn't usually around to notice.

Luckily, it wasn't the teacher who came through the door. Instead, another boy from my class made his way into the room.

The boy was a senior, and though we rarely spoke, I had been nursing a crush on him since the day we met. He looked like a modern teenage version of Jay Gatsby: elusive, mysterious, charismatic. He painted vibrant, psychedelic portraits of influential figures from the 1960s.

He'd done paintings of JFK and MLK and the man who popularized LSD. I imagined that after high school he would move to Seattle, or Tokyo, or Berlin. I guessed that when he wasn't painting, he was getting high on shrooms in the woods behind the school parking lot, attempting to catch glimpses of colors no one had ever seen before—but maybe he wasn't. My crushes on boys were often like that; I was swept up in ideas of them, and I rarely ever got close enough to learn the truth.

I gave the boy a nod, and he offered me the slightest smile in return.

Other students began filing into the classroom, hardly acknowledging one another. After a few minutes of shuffling, they turned their heads toward their half-finished artworks. Some students dipped their brushes into gooey paints. Others sharpened their pencils to slivers.

I was working on a piece mostly using charcoal. I liked the way the little black nubs left shadows all over my skin; I often showed up to my other classes with stains covering my arms and cheeks. The piece I had in progress was eventually going to depict an elaborate tent. One corner was finished. Black and white stripes swooped over the page, mimicking billowing peaks of fabric.

All art students were forced to pick a concentration: a theme unifying their work. My theme was the circus.

Maybe the circus was an obvious obsession. I was a

misfit and a recent runaway. I didn't like to admit it, but I missed home. I romanticized a place where starting over could be easier than it had been in real life. My dream-world was inhabited by an elephant who carefully tackled a tightrope and a dozen lonely clowns who wore ruffles and buttons. There were mimes and acrobats and animals, and a hundred other beautiful, decadent freaks. They lived on a stack of fancy papers inside the art studio's storage space.

The illustration I was working on was set to be a home for them all: an enormous big-top tent.

I smeared my thumb against the page, shading a fold in the tent's fabric. I was excited about the piece. The shapes were beginning to grow recognizable. I wasn't the best artist in the class by any means, but I was getting much better from all the extra lunch hours I had spent working in the studio.

The girl who normally sat across from me walked over. She took a closer peek at my drawing. She was one of the few acquaintances I had made in the weeks since moving to Colorado. She had soft, honey-colored hair, and her name sounded like it could have been the name of a new planet. As she hovered next to me, I felt a wave of nerves. I wanted her to like my drawing. For a few heartbeats, she looked on in silence.

"It's going to be a circus tent," I explained.

"Yeah, I can tell," she replied, smiling. I felt a glimmer of relief.

I paused my shading so I could take a look at the painting she had been working on. It was a watercolor portrait. A baby. She was talented. The baby's eyes looked so dewy and real, I thought they might start crying right on the page.

"Your piece is looking really good," I said.

"Thanks," she replied. "It's getting there. . . ."

She seemed like she was going to say something else, but then she just looked out the window. Watching her mind waltz somewhere outside the studio, I understood. It could be hard to talk about art. I knew certain feelings couldn't be translated from images into explanations.

Our teacher walked by, and we went back to working on our pieces. The faint smell of acrylic paint swept through the room. I watched the girl with the planet name gently color the baby's cheek peach pink. The cute senior boy had claimed rights to the classroom speaker, and he put on a moody playlist—Death Cab for Cutie and Bon Iver and Grizzly Bear. We all worked in time to the guitar strums. Every once in a while, a classmate or two felt bold enough to hum along.

Time passed quickly. The minutes felt like snapshots from a montage scene. I drew and erased and blended. Sweet, somber lyrics rippled through the room, and I tried to pretend I was living inside a movie. I tried to believe all the lonely moments were going to cut away to a joyful scene later on.

The bell rang just as I finished drawing the cascading curve of a fabric pleat. I forced myself to pack my charcoals away. I quickly rinsed some of the soot from my hands, and then I left the studio.

The hallway contracted as students poured from their classrooms. I tucked my hands beneath the straps of my backpack, and I clung to the walls. I tried my best to avoid the hallway traffic. I pretended the bittersweet guitar music was still playing in the background. I went through the motions of my other classes. I counted down the hours until I could return to the studio.

Nearly every day followed the same pattern: I ate lunch alone (sometimes allowing myself a cookie, sometimes barely managing to take bites of my sandwich); I chatted with the planet-named girl; I made up stories in my head about the boy who might or might not take drugs in his free time; I drew to the tempo of some hip, sad playlist he had put together. None of us were exactly friends, but we kept each other company, and we gave one another an audience, and that was good enough.

Some days, the girl with the planet name struck up conversations with me—mostly just small talk, but occasionally we let little shards of our true feelings slip out. She told me about her home life, which was complicated and sad. I told her about my constant misplacedness, which I tried to mask by counting calories and distracting myself with hunger. We kept each other's secrets well.

We drew, and painted, and erased. The melancholy music sucked us into a trancelike state. Sometimes, the lonely movie montage felt inescapable, but we still carried on. Eventually, I finished the drawing of the big-top tent. I stored it alongside my other sketches.

I humbly offered my circus freaks a home.

Here is another spoiler. A good one, I promise.

When I graduated from high school, I lost touch with almost everyone from my art class. I stopped drawing, and I abandoned my old illustrations. I stored them in my parents' basement, where they were left to collect dust. I forgot about the circus I had made. I tried to forget about all the days I spent wandering around that high school campus without a group of friends to eat lunch with.

Then one day, I saw the girl with the planet-sounding name. She popped into my social media feed, and curiosity bit my lip. I couldn't keep myself from scrolling through her history. I paged through weeks of pictures. I was careful not to accidentally leave traces of my investigation. I tapped across her profile with light fingers. I found out that she had moved to Boulder. She had gotten engaged. She had taken pictures with bronzing autumn leaves. And then—there was an announcement. A graduation. She had taken on her first job as a social worker. And I remembered all those portraits of babies and the moments we sat together in class, sharing secrets. For a brief minute, I felt like I had witnessed a small miracle. For a couple of blinks, my memories flooded back, and the world seemed to make sense.

Because of course she had become a social worker. Of course she looked after dewy-eyed babies just like the ones she once drew.

I thought about my own life and how it had changed since high school: I ended up working for a real circus. I toured around North America with Cirque du Soleil. I got to live among a gaggle of other runaways.

Our lives really did imitate our art.

And because I had once liked imagining stories about a boy in our class—the one who drew the extraordinary psychedelic portraits—I invented an ending for him as well: Once again, I imagined that he wandered into some Technicolor city, maybe Seattle, or Tokyo, or Berlin. I tried to picture him still painting, still unknowingly breaking the hearts of women he barely knew. I tried to will my daydreams into truth.

Back in high school, we were all strays, but I like to believe we were just living through a short, sad scene. I like to believe our lives had really been set to the perfect

13

Every Good Story Has a Prom Scene

I had a blue dress hanging in my closet. It was a bright, concentrated shade of blue, like a peacock's belly or a beetle's wing. The bust's fabric folded into glossy pleats.

A couple of times, I secretly unhooked the dress from its hanger and wore it while working on homework alone in my room. I imagined the act felt similar to putting on expensive lingerie—a bit romantic and a bit flirtatious and somehow slightly taboo. When I slipped into the dress, the strapless neckline paralleled the specific curves of my collarbones. The front of the skirt swept above my knees, and the back cascaded below my calves. It made me want to slink my recently shaved legs against one another like a fresh grasshopper.

It made me feel pretty.

My mom had bought the dress on an impulse. We were window-shopping at the mall when she saw it hanging on a mannequin. "It'll be perfect for prom," she said. I thought so too.

Despite the fact that I generally resented the culture of public high school, I always loved the idea of prom. I loved the notion of creating One Perfect Night. I grew teary-eyed at the cheesy dance scenes in movies—it didn't matter if the film was a 1980s classic or a low-budget indie flick. I was a sucker for a slow dance.

The trouble was, at my new school, I had no plans to go to prom.

Britney and I were eating lunch when an Edible Arrangement arrived at our front door. We had grown a bit more comfortable in one another's company, but our conversations remained cautious. We quietly compared notes on homework assignments and complained about how far away summer still seemed to be.

"Delivery for Britney," a man called into our home.

The gift had been sent by Luke, a baby-faced singles skater who went to our school. The gesture was both precious and performative, and it made our cheeks flush. I didn't want to admit my slight case of jealousy, so I pushed my green feelings down, and I clapped my hands together while Britney read the accompanying card: *Will you go to prom with me?*

We both cooed at the words. Britney quickly texted Luke to accept his invitation. She wasn't sure about their chemistry, but she was interested in the prospect of a night out and the allure of wearing her own fancy dress.

"You're planning on coming to prom too, right?" she asked me.

"Umm. I don't think so," I said. I couldn't hide my disappointment.

"Come on. You have to go!"

"I can't. I don't have a date. I don't even have a group of friends to go with."

Britney plucked a piece of chocolate-covered pineapple off a skewer and bit it in half.

"You can come with me and Luke. I don't think he'll mind!"

"He will! He likes you *a lot*." I gave an exaggerated look toward the Edible Arrangement and stole a plain strawberry from its bouquet. "And anyway, I don't want to be a third wheel."

"Maybe there's still time for us to find you a date?" she offered.

"I doubt it, but I guess we'll see," I said.

I wasn't keeping my hopes up. I had been through this charade before—every dance in my entire life had come and gone without any boys asking me to be their plus-one.

⌒

The first prom scene I ever fell in love with begins with another elaborate promposal. The scene is from the movie *High School Musical 3: Senior Year.*

Corbin Bleu's character stands on a table in the school cafeteria. He holds a small clump of flowers while the entire student body looks on. When his date confirms her attendance, Corbin exits the cafeteria and finds himself on a stage. Soon enough, everyone joins in an extravagant dance number. Zac Efron's character changes into a frilly powder-blue suit. Vanessa Hudgens's character carries a dress on a hanger, flicking it like a matador's cape. The girls take one side of the stage and the guys take the other. They chant lyrics dripping with tug-of-war playfulness: The girls sing of excitement; the boys sing of dread. But by the end of the number, every boy pairs off with a girl. The couples disco and jive into the night. They all flash exaggerated smiles when they hit their final poses.

The scene is an all-American heterosexual fever dream, and I grew up absolutely adoring it.

⌒

Jason Brown moved into our basement a few days after the Edible Arrangement showed up. Matt had gotten his own apartment (where he could have more privacy and throw parties to his heart's content), and Jason arrived to fill his place.

I knew of Jason before he ever became my roommate. He was a phenomenal skater—known for his charismatic performance skills and his trademark ponytail. He was just coming off a silver-medal win at the World Junior Figure Skating Championships in Milan. I was left a bit starstruck when I found out he was going to be living in our house.

Jason showed up with his parents late on a Friday night. Britney had been spending the weekend with her moms in Denver again, so I answered when the doorbell rang. I caught a glimpse of his familiar frame through the window. He looked exactly the same as he did on TV, except instead of a skating costume, he wore glasses and a hoodie. His chin and cheekbones were shaded with a light brown stubble. His hair was collected into the famous wavy ponytail.

By the time the door was fully open, I could hear his voice overflowing into the room.

"Oh my gosh! You must be Karina! It's so nice to meet you!" His sentences all arrived as exclamations. Normally I would have been overwhelmed by someone so energetic and extroverted, but I was surprisingly comforted by his manner. I could tell, just instants after meeting him, that his joy was both genuine and infectious.

"Hi!" I said back, letting my own voice skip.

Jason wrapped me in a hug. His parents were quick to follow.

I helped them carry a few suitcases inside, and when they were settled, we all chatted together on the couch. Jason had just graduated from high school in Chicago—and like me, he had moved to Colorado so he could train in a more elite skating environment. He had already spent several years on Team USA, and I wanted to know every detail of that experience. He told me about his most recent competitions and his latest travels, and I listened with wholehearted wonder. His stories were magnetic, and they made me remember why I had moved in the first place. I spilled a few dry facts about myself, but I mostly let Jason do the talking. I felt relieved that he had a lot to say. His enthusiasm tempered my shyness.

In the following days, Jason and I became friends in a rare, immediate way. I spent every moment with him and his family—tagging along when they went to the grocery store, and sharing hiking trails in the nearby mountains. For the first time since moving away from home, I felt close with someone who wasn't on the other side of a state line.

At the end of the weekend, Jason's parents flew to Chicago and Britney returned from Denver.

When Britney walked in from the garage, she startled. Jason and I had been hanging out together, singing along to a playlist of his sister's favorite hip-hop songs. Britney was accustomed to my ghostly quiet, so she was surprised by the sound of my voice pouring uninhibitedly from our living room.

Around one another, Britney and I had both been really timid, but Jason's presence seemed to dissolve all our previous reservations. That afternoon, the three of us talked for hours, laughing and sharing and joking as if we were old friends. We sat around our kitchen table, playfully shoving each other's shoulders and gripping one another's arms during the good bits of our stories. I found myself talking without testing any sentences inside my head first. I barely fidgeted. Outside, the sun dimmed behind the mountains. We didn't even notice when the room went dark. We didn't even notice when snow began falling.

"It's amazing, this life we're about to start," Jason said. "No adults. Just the three of us. It feels like we're living in a coming-of-age story."

His full-hearted optimism made me want to agree.

A few days later, Britney ran downstairs to grab her car keys. Her prom dress was tucked inside a plastic bag and draped over her arms. It billowed and bounced behind her like a heavy kite while she raced around. She was leaving to go shoe shopping, and she wanted to bring the dress to ensure that her whole prom ensemble would match. Jason and I had been sitting on the couch, watching TV. Before Britney ran out the door, she stopped in her tracks, as if she had forgotten something. She slowly turned to look at us.

"Oh my god!" she squealed. "You two should go to prom together. It'll be perfect! We can all make dinner reservations together, and we can take pictures as a group!"

"Um . . . are you sure Luke is going to want that?" I asked with ample hesitation.

"He won't mind!" she insisted. "It'll be more fun this way. It will take the pressure off the two of us!"

I worked up the courage to look over at Jason. Even though we had been getting along well, we still hardly knew each other. I didn't want to make him uncomfortable. It seemed in poor taste to force my new roommate into being my last-minute date.

Luckily, Jason didn't seem fazed. He smiled at me and shrugged.

"Sounds like it could be fun," he said.

I let out a giggle of joy.

"Looks like we're going to prom!" I said. "I actually already have this dress in my closet," I added.

I ran upstairs to grab the dress. Britney and I both left to go shoe shopping. I felt a pang of worthiness. It suddenly occurred to me that part of the appeal of dating was getting to be seen as half of a couple. It didn't matter to me that Jason and I were only going as friends—what mattered was that people would view me as part of a pair. I would look like I belonged with someone.

The big night was quickly approaching, so we had to plan everything quickly. In the following days, Jason rented a tux from a shop across the street, and he dug a pair of oxfords from his closet. I hastily reserved our tickets and painted my nails. I believed that like all major life occasions, this event called for a soundtrack, so I built a prom-day playlist.

The morning of the dance, Jason and I shared a pair of headphones, and I streamed my playlist while we walked to the grocery store together. I bought Jason a boutonniere, and in turn he bought me a corsage. The store was sold out of everything except bright yellow flowers, so we went with those. The whole week had already been charged with a series of joyful exclamations of the phrase *Why not!*

I relished our hipster-like approach. We weren't overthinking things; the casualness of it all made me feel calm and cool for one of the first times in my life. But in truth, I also couldn't hide my shameless excitement. I was thrilled to have a date and to get the chance to wear my blue dress. I was overjoyed to carry out the ridiculous high school tradition. The day of prom, I got to exist somewhere inside a rare middle space: the space between the alternative and the mainstream, the space between eagerness and apathy, the impossible, delicious space that could make my unnamed differentness feel livable.

When I was in middle school, I unabashedly loved the movie *Twilight*—especially the prom scene at the end.

In the scene, Kristen Stewart's and Robert Pattinson's characters slow-dance in a gazebo together. She's wearing a blue dress, the gazebo twinkles with a million fairy lights, and the couple has somehow managed to isolate themselves from all the other students. They hover in a perfect moment. An Iron & Wine song plays softly in the background. The whole setting is marked by syrupy passion. The characters end the movie by wistfully dreaming of a lifetime together.

For a long while, I considered the scene to be the epitome of romance.

But a few years after watching *Twilight* on the big screen, I saw another Kristen Stewart movie: *The Runaways*. I secretly watched the film one afternoon while the rest of my family attended a soccer tournament on the other side of town.

The Runaways depicts an entirely different kind of passion. It tells the story of an all-girl rock band. Kristen Stewart portrays a teenage Joan Jett. There is no prom scene. There are no fairy lights. No gazebo. Instead, the movie lives inside a world marked by its roughness. In her first appearance on-screen, Kristen Stewart's character buys a leather jacket. In her second scene, she kisses a girl. By the end of the movie, she's an international rock star.

The leather-jacket kiss was the first lesbian kiss I can ever remember seeing on-screen.

And I remember believing—for a very long time—that there were only two kinds of love. There could be a man, and a prom, and a gazebo, or there could be a woman, and a leather jacket, and a rock band.

And I felt an undeniable tug toward both. But at sixteen, I believed the world was made up of choices, and I didn't fully understand that I was *already* living inside a gray area, and I owned a blue prom dress, but I didn't own a leather jacket yet.

And at sixteen, I never considered what it might look like to meld two story lines together.

~

Getting ready took a few hours. I curled my hair and glossed my lips. In those days, I had only a few skills in the world of beauty—I grew up right before the booming era of makeup tutorials, and I was too embarrassed to ask my mom to teach me how to wing my eyeliner—so I had to make do with the few tricks I had. I could twist my hair into ringlets. I could mascara my lashes black. By the time I was done, I felt accomplished.

Britney and I made a big show of walking down the stairs in our dresses. It was cheesy and clichéd, and we knew it, but that didn't stop us.

Luke was waiting at the bottom of the stairs. He was nervous. His cheeks were dimpled and red. Britney smiled with the confidence of knowing that she was the object of an enormous crush. Jason and I spied on the pair; we knew we would be entertained by their hesitant flirtations all night.

The four of us took pictures in our front yard. Luke gingerly placed his hands against Britney's waist. Jason and I giggled through our poses, and we snapped a bunch of selfies between the highly staged shots. Britney's parents kept corralling us together for *only a few more.* When we were done, we crowded into Jason's car.

I'm having fun, I thought.

We ate dinner at the seafood restaurant where Matt worked. We showed up during his shift, and he brought us some fruity mocktails on the house (our little group followed the rules too rigidly to try to score ourselves some real booze). Jason initiated a dramatic toast, and we all raised our glasses into the air.

When the menus came, I pretended to look through the columns of items. I had developed a habit of searching for calorie counts online before heading to restaurants. I ordered a plate of salmon and stared down at my dress. I prayed the fish and the drinks wouldn't alter its fit. I resolved to dance a bit extra to burn away the calories from the meal. I tapped my foot on the tiled floor. It was becoming harder and harder to collect happy memories. Worries about food always crawled in. (I wish I could leave these parts out, but this is how things really happened.)

Luckily, Jason interrupted my intrusive thoughts.

"Who's ready to head to the dance?" he asked, his voice all excitement and bliss.

In the car, I sat shotgun next to Jason. Britney and Luke sat together in the back seat. I tried to peek through the rearview mirror to see if the bashful pair was holding hands, but I couldn't quite tell. Jason noticed my efforts. He looked through the rearview mirror himself and nodded discreetly. We smiled at one another from the corners of our eyes, and I felt relieved to be out of the restaurant and headed to the dance.

Jason rolled the sunroof back and turned the speakers up all the way. We felt a sense of comradery. For one night, we gloried in the ability to indulge in wildly normal lives. Skating had always taken up so much space for all of us that we hardly ever got to feel like teenagers in the movies and TV shows, who were allowed to care about football games and dances instead of Grand Prix assignments and rhinestone costumes. But for this one night, things were different. Even though Luke had been fairly quiet all evening, he joined us in singing. I could feel something wonderful spilling from our voices. The highway air whipped against our faces as we raced across the night.

By the time we arrived at the dance, we were fashionably late, wind-shaken, and blissful. Our timing was perfect, though, because the dance floor had already warmed itself up.

Britney and I led our dates by the hand, and we gripped one another with our spare arms. The four of us toppled into the crowd, making space for ourselves somewhere inside the strobing lights and silky dresses. The DJ played a song that instructed everyone on the dance floor to put their hands up, and we did. Hundreds of arms flew skyward at once. We jumped and shook the floor with tremendous thuds. I caught a glimpse of my art-class crush clutching a girl who must have been his date. They both smiled at me, and then they threw their arms in the air. The roomful of flailing limbs belonged to everyone, and the beats belonged to all of us.

In the dim lighting, I hardly recognized any of the faces surrounding me. To be fair, I hardly knew anyone at the school to begin with, but we seemed so different without our sweatshirts and jeans and messy buns. The formalwear changed us. I swear everyone became a better version of themselves that night—a version that was a little kinder, a little more whole. I felt anonymous in a good way . . . in a way that felt like being a part of something.

I grabbed Jason by the shoulders, and I moved his hands to my sides. We pressed our hips together, and our bodies rocked like they knew what they were doing—like our knees and hips and chests had taken over. Like the axis of the earth had also begun to sway. And Jason and I danced like we had somehow been practicing our whole lives.

It amazed me how my body—the same body that I had stared down at with worry at dinner—could be the body that was now bouncing in the crowd. It didn't seem real: that one minute I could be shrinking and the next grinding and swooping and expanding across the room. Maybe I only hated my body when I kept it too still for too long. Maybe bodies were only meant to be seen under strobe lights. When I was moving, my edges disappeared. I became a part of the room. A reflection of the light. I filled with color. My dress fit perfectly.

I kept dancing. Eventually, my hands found Britney's hips, and hers found my shoulders. We rocked together too. Luke and Jason left to grab us glasses of water, but Britney and I couldn't bring ourselves to stray from the dance floor for even a single breath.

Handfuls of the students wandered outside. They moved on toward their limousines and their after-parties, but the four of us held out until the very end. The DJ dedicated the last song to the lovebirds—that awful Aerosmith song that plays during every school dance—only it wasn't quite as awful as it usually was. I danced with Jason in a close embrace. It was the kind of easy cuddle that suggested we were destined to be friends. We peered over every few beats to playfully sneak peeks at Luke and Britney. They probably weren't meant for each other, but it was still sweet to watch them slow-dance.

The whole room of people step-tapped in perfect synchronization.

I thought: *Heaven might be a dance floor.* And then the lights flashed on, and I saw my new friends standing next to me, and I saw my own body in the perfect blue dress, and I squinted my eyes from the sudden brightness, and everyone filed toward the doors.

Heaven just might be a dance floor, I thought again, and I walked away with the rest of the crowd.

Right before moving to Colorado, I went to see the movie *The Perks of Being a Wallflower* with my friends. The movie contains a prom scene that is not quite a prom scene; it's technically a homecoming dance.

The scene begins with the enticing violin notes of the song "Come On Eileen." Emma Watson's character dances, uninhibitedly, with Ezra Miller's character. Ezra Miller's character is openly gay. The pair ends up having more fun at the dance than anyone. Their joy is palpable. They kick and spin and shake together. There is no romance or back-and-forth of desire or unfulfilled need to be a part of a couple. There is no promposal, or gazebo, or leather jacket. Mostly, there is just unrestrained dancing.

I remember leaving the theater aspiring to the same kind of joy. I thought that I had witnessed the perfect prom scene.

But as I left my own prom, I thought I had lived a moment that was even sweeter.

14

A Brief Piece of Advice

I have something to confess: I hate writing about my eating disorder.

I don't like transcribing the gritty details. I don't enjoy piecing together tales of my restricting. In fact, my mind will hardly let me remember the hungriest moments. There are weeks and months of my life that have been carved away. I can dig up memories from a year ago, and I can uncover memories from two years ago. Even three or four years back, my mind can keep following the exactness of certain colors and textures and smells. But at some point, the path disappears. When I reach toward certain sections of my history, my hands come up empty.

Memory is a kind of reliving, and no part of me wants to go back.

Amid the haze, though, there are a few evenings that stand out. I know that I cannot truly tell my story without brushing up against the somber reality of these nights.

Here is some advice: Proceed with care.

Years ago—when I was especially lonely and especially sad—I used to look up eating-disorder stories on the internet. I googled *anorexia books,* and then I read every summary and review that I could find. I researched countless food diaries published on blogs. I uncovered poems that had been written by professional thin girls. Occasionally, I'd watch clips of YouTube documentaries. All the documentaries were the same: dramatic images of hip bones, stifled tears. I tried to feed myself on the images of other people's untouched plates.

I took mental notes while consuming these stories. I learned how to suppress my hunger in a thousand creative ways. It's a difficult thing to explain. . . . Why would I make things worse? Why would I take on other people's bad habits when I already had so many of my own?

I still don't have all the answers. The best explanation I can offer is that watching these videos and reading these stories felt like wiggling a loose tooth. Hunger felt like a pain I could press my tongue up against. I was scared that without the hunger—without the tangible hurt—I would be left with a gap.

If you reached for this book because you wanted to press yourself up against a specific kind of heartache, I get it. I've been there, but that is not what this story is for. I am not here to offer you creative new tactics for starving or shrinking.

I am here to offer you this: If my book ever makes you want to measure out your meals, please close its covers. If any chapter ever makes you want to erase your body, please put these pages down and go have a snack. If you are looking for more ways to harm yourself, pay attention to me now: I love you.

I want you to learn how to love yourself.

I am going to share some stories of my eating disorder, but if you insist on taking notes, don't focus on the ways I harmed myself. Focus on the resilience of my body, and the reasons I got better, and the joy I found after I let my hunger fizzle out like the slow dissipation of bubbles in a bath. If you take anything away from this story, take away a feeling of hope.

Take away the pleasant calm that remains.

15

Proof My Body Loved Me Even When I Didn't Love It Back

By the time fall rolled around in Colorado Springs, I had developed a love-hate relationship with skating practices. Jonathan and I were preparing for sectionals. Since ice-dance events tend to draw fewer competitors than singles events, we did not have to compete at the regional championships. Instead, the top four teams at sectionals would move on to the national championships, and I made it my mission to ensure that we would be among those teams.

My mind devoured ice dancing. It thirsted for the sport. We trained for three to four hours on the ice every day, and I spent the majority of that time untangling the nuances of technique and wrestling the details of my body. I obsessed over the line that traced from my hip to my knee to my toe while my leg was extended. I learned how to arch my head away from Jonathan's arms so I looked like I was being permanently swayed by an imaginary wind. I engaged the muscles in my core so I could balance over the sweet spot of my blades and continue turning for as long as I wanted.

I attempted to eat less and less—it seemed like such a natural decision. Jonathan was a relatively small guy, and I believed that the smaller I made myself, the easier I would be to lift. I reached for every advantage I could find. Besides, everyone seemed to equate my weight loss with my continuous improvement.

What have you been doing? What's your secret? I wish I had your self-control.

While my mind sought comfort in the obsessive nature of training, my body grew tired of the scrutiny. It exhausted itself. During some practices, I lost all feeling in my fingertips. My calves cramped because my muscles had been deprived of nutrients. Skating elements that had once been easy grew harder to execute. When practices ended, I slept for hours on end. I told myself that these were just the normal side effects of elite athletics. But deep down, I knew better: I could hear when my stomach rumbled, and I simply refused to listen.

While I slumped around my house in the afternoons, the words *eating disorder* and *anorexia* reared themselves

126

in my brain. They seemed to curl and loop through my subconscious in cursive neon letters. I would often think the words without any association or context. They simply lit up my neurons like the sudden flicker of a screen saver.

I tried to blink the thoughts back. I didn't feel like I qualified for an eating disorder yet—at least, not what I considered to be *enough* of one.

My body was not emaciated. My thighs were thick, and unless I stood at very specific angles, they smooshed together beneath the skirts of my skating dresses. My stomach never looked entirely flat, despite the fact that I crunched through hundreds of sit-ups while nobody was looking. My cheeks hollowed a little, but they didn't lose all their baby fat. My BMI never dropped into the underweight category. But above all else, I consumed far more calories than I believed people with *real* eating disorders did. I ate carefully planned snacks and bagged lunches and dinners weighed out in measuring cups. I resented the fact that I ate, but I still ate all the time.

In fact, the more I tried to forget about food, the more I seemed to get sucked into memories of flavor and fullness.

One morning, I woke up to what I swore was the buzz of my alarm. I had been dreaming about breakfast: eggs, pancakes, thick slices of bacon that rippled and curled. Syrup had soaked through the pancakes; fat had dripped from the meat. In reality, I planned to eat something else entirely: a carefully weighed bowl of oatmeal, black coffee, and maybe a piece of fruit. And yet my body still looked forward to its breakfast. My taste buds would take whatever they could get.

After forcing myself out of bed, I made my way downstairs to the kitchen and drank a full glass of water while I zoned out, watching the oatmeal turn and turn under the yellow light of the microwave. My house felt quieter than normal. My roommates were still asleep, along with the rest of the world. Outside the living room window, I could hear the quiet howl of an early-autumn wind.

I remember the house being cold that morning, but then again, I remember feeling cold often—partly because I had not gotten used to Colorado's weather changes and partly because my body had lost some of its insulation.

I paused the microwave before it beeped and threatened to wake my roommates. I stared down at my oatmeal. I ate slowly, as if smaller bites would fill my stomach further. Sips of black coffee divided the time between mouthfuls. The spoon grazed the bottom of the bowl. The scraping matched the sound of longing. I took some comfort in the little torturous rituals.

I thought the words *I hate myself.*

I thought them so easily. As if the sentence was not violent. I thought the words just as casually as I had thought about the cool weather outside. Then I finished my breakfast.

After slipping my dishes into the dishwasher, I walked

back upstairs to get dressed. I put on a pair of leggings. I yawned. I checked my phone so I could immediately start counting down the hours before my next meal. My phone screen read 2:47—which couldn't be right. I wasn't supposed to wake up until six. I checked the screen again: 2:48.

The house had been unnervingly quiet for a reason. My body had woken me up in the middle of the night and convinced me that it was time to eat. My stomach couldn't bear the lustful, empty dreams any longer—it was so hungry, it took matters into its own hands.

I immediately sighed with annoyance. I felt tricked by the unplanned calories.

With my realization of the time, an exhaustion swept over me. I changed back into my pajamas and double-checked that I had set a proper alarm. I listened to the wind outside, hoping its cavernous hum could lull me back to sleep.

My body hates me back, I thought just before the dark took over.

But once I fell asleep again, something beautiful happened. I didn't dream about food. I got a few precious hours of peace. I was offered an escape from the aching life I had constructed.

When my alarm beeped later—my real alarm—I shook myself from my bed. I felt rested in a way I had not felt in months.

I made myself another bowl of oatmeal. I resolved to eat breakfast all over again.

I had generally imagined my existence as a battle between my body and my mind. I pictured *hate* as a beach ball, volleying back and forth between my brain and my cellulite. But I was wrong. My body was trying to save me.

There were always parts of me fighting to show myself tenderness—my stomach when it rumbled, my calves when they cramped, my brain when it conjured dreams about food. That night, all my cells worked together to wake me up and convince me to eat another meal.

There was no divide between my body and my mind at all. There was only the whole of me, struggling to find survival and grace.

When I didn't dream about food, I often dreamed of my friends from back home. The dreams were languid and shimmery. They were dipped in night colors and cloying mist.

In the dreams, my friends and I scrunched into Mackenzie's car and drove toward Arizona's empty desert spaces. We sped along a freeway until we found a patch of dirt that was barren of cacti and creatures. We pulled a picnic blanket from the car's trunk, and then we each grabbed handfuls of fabric and stretched the threads wide before we pressed the blanket against the earth. Our bodies draped themselves onto the ground, and our gazes turned skyward. Then we watched meteorites fall through the night air. Bits of stardust tumbled and skittered, only to be consumed by the desert's crackled sand. Some of the rocks fell so close to us, we could feel the winds of their descent whistle past our ears, but we were never struck. The crashes exhilarated us. We hugged one another when the sparks singed our hair. We traced our initials into the glistening dust that scattered across the picnic blanket.

We had found the middle space between the sky and the ground.

We tried to take pictures of the star chunks right before they landed, but trying to capture them was like trying to take a picture of the moon—both hopeful and ineffective.

I always woke up from the dreams feeling a little bit loved and a little bit vacant.

I always woke up from the dreams feeling just like the moment someone lets go of a hug.

16

No Need to Hit Rock Bottom

A glowy-cheeked baby bounced in Britney's lap. A toddler with messy curls snuggled between me and Jason. The little girls were the daughters of a local skating coach. We had all agreed to spend our Saturday night babysitting.

Our TV played an animated film that was saturated in a pallete of pink and purple hues. The toddler had selected the movie: It was about a lonely unicorn who gets transformed into a woman. I was the only one who was really paying any attention to its finer plot points. Jason and Britney were busy cooing at the baby.

Britney was a natural with the little ones. She held the baby with an ease that I envied—she was one of those girls who seem to have been born with perfect instincts for mothering. Jason was a pretty good babysitter too. He knew how to make the toddler belly-giggle just by making a funny face. In comparison, my caretaking skills seemed clumsy. I liked kids, but they made me nervous. They looked so vulnerable. Caring for them felt like watching tadpoles swim near the edge of a cliff.

The toddler started to get antsy, and we asked her if she wanted to pause the movie. "What do you want to do next? We could make dinner?"

"Yes!" the toddler said without hesitation.

"Dinner it is!" Britney announced.

Jason shot me a look—a look that said, *Please eat with us.*

Jason had confronted me a few days earlier, after I had spent yet another evening picking at a bag of popcorn instead of making myself a real dinner.

"Do you want to talk about whatever's going on?" he had asked, looking at me and then at the half-empty bag of popcorn.

I *had* wanted to talk about it, but in the moment, I chickened out. It was similar to the first time I tried to describe a panic attack; I couldn't form the right sentences. A guilt tugged at my words: I knew other people—people all over the world—had bigger problems and harder lives.

I didn't want to admit that my pain was somewhat self-inflicted. I didn't want to make a big deal out of problems I had seemingly caused. It was a truth that often felt too shameful to explain.

I don't know why I do this to myself, I thought.

I ended up telling Jason I was okay. I told him not to worry, and my life was able to carry on as usual.

Britney walked into the kitchen and helped the toddler wash her fumbly hands. Jason stared at me with a cautious sense of expectation. I clenched my jaw out of reflex, and I moved toward the sink to wash my hands too.

We started cooking, letting tortillas warm in the bottom of a pan and sautéing ground beef with a half dozen seasonings. The toddler helped sprinkle lettuce over our plates in confetti shreds. I palmed a tomato that I was about to slice into disks. The room filled with the smells of chili powder and onions and salt. The kitchen warmed the way kitchens do when they're busy—charged with the energy of bodies and their hunger. I inhaled deeply, and I pretended the experience of being around food was the same as consuming it. This, of course, wasn't true. After months of trying to live off smells of food and dreams of food and thoughts of food, I knew nothing could substitute for taste. A thought couldn't fill my belly. A smell couldn't take the hunger away.

The baby started to fuss, so Jason heated a bottle in the microwave while we cooked.

After a half hour of dancing around the kitchen, we sat down to eat. The four of us circled our small table, and the baby peeked over the edge of her playpen to watch. The toddler's taco fillings spilled out of the sides. She took big bites, letting her cheeks stain messy with salsa, while I ate in a slow, measured way, avoiding eye contact. I fidgeted with the food on my plate. I was so hungry, though. Usually when I ate, I stuck with the same boring staples: sugar-free Jell-O, baby carrots, low-fat soups. Any deviations from my strict diet felt like tugging on a lose thread. This was my fear: If I let myself have better foods—real, heavy, mess-making foods—I would spiral. I would be tempted by the flavors I had once loved.

While I picked at my plate, the trail of spices led me away from the careful calorie counting that echoed in my head. I wasn't a perfect anorexic; I didn't stop myself. I ate a whole taco, then another, then another. I laughed with Jason as the toddler tried to give Britney a sticky hug. I licked my fingers instead of wiping them on a napkin. My life briefly felt normal. Britney and Jason both seemed relieved.

Together, we all cleared the table. I stood at the sink, rinsing dishes. Jason scooped the leftovers into mismatched Tupperware containers. Britney picked up the baby and rocked her in her arms. The toddler waddled through the living room.

"I'll be back in a minute," I said. I finished clearing the last dish and headed toward the bathroom. A fullness had set in that I was not accustomed to; I swore I could feel the weight of every bite that was now sitting in my stomach. The moments of peace I had felt just seconds before were disrupted by frightening waves of guilt.

I walked into my bathroom. The walls were a distinct shade of orange. I had left a pile of dirty clothes tossed on the floor and the shower curtain hurled open. Somehow, the small space felt harsher than usual. I locked the door and looked into the mirror.

This is where my memory fails me: I can't be sure of how I really looked that night. I can only recall the strange, hallucinatory version of my reflection. I remember seeing a face that did not look like my own face. I remember seeing a body that I hardly recognized as my own body. My skin took on a yellowish quality. My outline seemed to waver, like bubble gum stretching and shrinking from the exhale and inhale of a soft breath. I thought I might fall out of my skin. I had no idea where my body began and ended. The reflection seemed to offer proof—I was malleable and unstable. I was not in command of anything at all.

I collapsed onto the floor. The bath mat pressed up against my face. I didn't cry. Something about the eating disorder muted my emotions—which was part of the appeal. I didn't have to feel sad or even scared. Just exhausted. Just heavy.

The toddler's little voice rose from downstairs. She was babbling about something, but I couldn't understand her.

"Karina," Britney called up from the living room. "Are you coming back?"

"Yeah," I said. "I'll be down in a bit."

I remained horizontal along the bathroom floor. I thought about rock bottom.

Some nights when I couldn't sleep, I imagined what it would be like. I thought maybe rock bottom would hit me in a gray-tiled hospital room somewhere after I'd been forced to seek treatment. Or that rock bottom would make me look like the girls in eating-disorder movies—gaunt, standing pale and naked on a glass scale that displayed numbers in the double digits. Or that rock bottom would look like the skaters at the ice rink who were better than me at both skating and dieting.

But I also knew I wasn't anywhere near these invisible finish lines.

My body was not gaunt and double-digited. I showed up to most skating practices wearing two sports bras because my boobs remained bigger than almost every other athlete's. My roommates noticed the way I cut down my meals, but to an outsider, I would have looked fine, probably even "healthy." I still ate all the time—I just skipped dinner here and there; I just whittled down my snacks to simpler forms. For the most part, I never really considered myself sick enough to urgently need to get better.

While I lay on the bathroom floor, I fantasized again about rock bottom—a moment when things got so bad that someone else would flat out tell me to start taking care of myself. It was maddening the way I constantly needed permission, the way I wanted concern but hated actually receiving it. . . .

Britney yelled from downstairs.

"Come on, Karina. We're waiting for you!"

"Okay," I said. "I'll be right there."

I got up from the floor. I threw the pile of dirty clothes into a hamper. I went downstairs to play with the kids. I could tell that Britney was frustrated by my disappearance, and I didn't want to disappoint the toddler, who had been patiently waiting for me.

As I descended the stairs, the toddler stomped her clumsy feet.

Britney threw me a questioning look, but I pretended not to notice. I sat on the floor next to the toddler and silently stared at my stomach, feeling like a fraud, wondering if I really deserved to think the word "anorexia" as often as I did. Who was I to claim such a thing while my belly was perfectly full?

Jason put on some children's music. He picked up the baby and started bopping and shimmying to the rhythms. Britney grabbed hands with the toddler and twirled. They all sang along to "The Wheels on the Bus." I stayed on the floor and watched their improvised performance. They skipped. They stretched their arms wide. They threw their heads back while making all the designated bus-themed gestures. Britney hoisted the baby into the air, and she babbled as if she was singing along to the song.

"The kids are good with choreography. These little ones are going to be great skaters one day," Britney remarked.

No, I thought. *Skating will only make them hate themselves. Being a girl is hard enough already. . . .*

I didn't say the words out loud, but there they were in my mind, offering me a glimpse of the most devastating rock bottom. It wasn't a hospital room or a number on a scale. It wasn't my hip bones sharpened into points. It wasn't someone begging me to eat dessert. In fact, rock bottom had almost nothing to do with me.

Instead, rock bottom looked like another generation plagued by similar demons. Rock bottom would be the day the toddler went on her first diet. Rock bottom would be the day that the baby struggled to recognize herself in the mirror.

Maybe the cycle had already started. Had the girls noticed the way I picked at my plate? Had they paid attention to the way I stared down at the button of my jeans, the same way that I had paid attention to the skaters I admired? Were they going to copy me someday? Would the girls grow up to believe their aching was never worthy of being quelled?

A heat rose from the soles of my feet. I stood up to

sing and dance along with Jason and Britney and the little ones. We cycled through a number of short children's melodies. We performed for one another as if we were standing on a stage.

In the middle of a rousing rendition of "Twinkle, Twinkle, Little Star," the toddler let out a big, uninhibited yawn.

"Looks like it's almost time for bed," Britney said. The baby blinked her sleepy eyelids like she understood.

We put the unicorn movie on again while the kids drifted off. Within a matter of minutes, both girls were asleep. The toddler dreamed with her arms clutched around her body in a permanent hug. The baby's pinkie finger twitched. Her hair floated away from her head like dandelion wishes. The girls seemed entirely at peace.

I dutifully watched the ending of the movie. It was a happy ending: The unicorn-turned-woman transforms back into a mystical creature, and she finds a family of other creatures like her.

As the credits rolled, the coach arrived to pick up her daughters, and we hugged the little girls goodbye.

After the door clicked shut, Jason, Britney, and I sank into the couch together. We sat silently for a few beats, stifling our own yawns. Before I could second-guess myself, I forced a sentence out of my mouth.

"Umm . . . can I talk to you guys?" I said.

"Yeah. Always. Of course," they replied.

As much as I dig into my memory, I can't recall exactly

what I said next. Maybe I said something along the lines of *I don't want this to be my life anymore.* Or maybe I said, *I am tired of being hungry and sad.* Or maybe all I said was *I need help.* I just know that I said *something* out loud.

Before Britney or Jason could respond, my entire nervous system stirred like a limb prickling with pins and needles. My emotions snapped alive, and my numbness gave way to instinct. I inhaled a few deep breaths. It felt good to take oxygen from a room and not worry if it was more than I deserved. For so long, I had forgotten what it was like to feel anything but heaviness.

Britney and Jason listened to me. They let me hold their hands. They told me they would help me hide my bathroom scale.

And the images of rock bottom faded slightly, slipping away from my view.

Another spoiler.

My eating disorder did not go away by the time I woke up the next morning. I did not open my eyes wanting to kiss my belly rolls and caress the place where my thighs touch together. I didn't stop hating myself overnight.

I couldn't even bring myself to get professional help right away. I was terrified of the stigma, and I knew treatment could be expensive. But I was lucky, and I eventually got access to the resources I needed.

For a long time, I woke up missing the comfort of hunger. I missed the rush of feeling godlike and unneedy.

I would be lying if I did not admit that sometimes when my heart aches, and when my panic creeps up, and when I feel weighed down by all the hurting in the world, I still hear a clawing voice that sounds something like this: *The world would be better off with less of me.*

It's hard to pin down exactly where this voice comes from.

The voice belongs to me, but it seems to also belong to an ugly history that traces back to a time long before I was born—a history full of women who have been silenced, and queer people who have been erased, and bodies like mine (and bodies so very different from mine!) that have not been given the space to exist.

Here is the good news: As time goes on, I hear the starving thoughts less and less. Instead, I've learned to tap into a different set of voices.

Now when I feel a pull toward smallness, I try to listen to the whispers of people who have fought back. I try my best to tune in to the words of women in my sport who made room for themselves: Fumie Suguri, who was the first queer female skater I ever heard of; and Rachel Parsons, who competed with me while we were both struggling with our sexualities and our bodies; and Gracie Gold, who left the skating world to seek treatment for an eating disorder and then returned to prove that she could find success without shrinking herself. I try to listen to the voices of activists who fought for my right to be openly and wholly myself: the Uruguayan queer folks who made their homeland the second Latin American country to recognize same-sex marriage, and the trans women of color at Stonewall who are the reason we have Pride, and all the queer people who have lived quiet, gentle lives of survival. I try to listen to my mother, and my friends, and the women I fall for, who all tell me I am worthy of love and space.

I try to honor these people. I allow myself to need their help, and I do my best to make their voices louder than the destructive thoughts that I used to hold on to.

This is how I avoid rock bottom. We avoid it together.

If you are someone who also feels tempted to make your own body disappear, pay attention to me now: I love you.

You might not know how to take care of yourself yet, but I promise to be another voice amid the chorus, guiding you away from the shrinking you've inherited, guiding you toward a world where we don't feel ashamed of everything that we need.

If you or someone you know is struggling with an eating disorder, please visit the National Eating Disorder Association's website for help, or call their hotline at (800)-931-2237. nationaleatingdisorders.org

17

Halloween

Britney, Jason, and I grew closer and closer. We stayed up late together, talking to each other about our lives on the ice: Jason was hoping to land a spot on the Olympic team by the end of the year, and he was feeling a lot of added pressure. Britney was recovering from shoulder surgery, and she was frustrated by the long road to recovery. I was still trying to figure out how to continue training with a partner who remained the same size as my body slowly learned to fluctuate. We gave each other pep talks, and we vented about our coaches, and we continued to survive the frigid rinks.

Most of the time, though, we avoided talking about

skating. When we were at home, we were more concerned with other matters—like homework, and relationships, and figuring out what we were going to do with the rest of our lives. Without the constant interference of adults, we could fully commit to the chaos of our own evolution.

When Halloween rolled around, we decided to carve pumpkins in our living room. We laid down newspapers and sank our hands into our pumpkins' slushy insides. Orange stains covered our arms all the way up to our elbows. I blasted a playlist of rock bands that made me feel a little edgier and bolder than I usually felt. Trick-or-treaters knocked at our door and peeked inside our living room. We tossed huge handfuls of candy into their pillow-cases. Standing on the other side of the doorbell, we felt so grown-up, celebrating however we wanted and relish-ing the unconventional family we had built for ourselves. Britney toasted pumpkin seeds in the oven, and our house filled with the scent of cinnamon sugar.

As the sky got darker and fewer trick-or-treaters arrived at our house, our pumpkins hollowed out. The expressions of their jack-o'-lantern faces took shape. Newspapers held chunks we had carved away.

Britney and Jason playfully debated the existence of ghosts.

And while I put the finishing touches on my pump-kin masterpiece, I realized I wasn't lonely anymore. I was happy. It was the kind of feeling that comes from standing on a rooftop at night, or riding in a crowded car with the windows down, or stepping into the ocean with bare feet. The lack of emptiness was like realizing I had outgrown a pair of shoes—I didn't even notice that my life was shifting until the shift had already taken place. Without warning or ceremony, Colorado had become my new home.

My playlist shuffled to another song, a quieter ballad. We began cleaning up pumpkin guts and newspapers from our floor. The sidewalks of our neighborhood emptied, but I could still hear cars headed somewhere.

As a kid growing up in the desert, I had always been surrounded by cacti and dust, but that year, I got to watch leaves change color. One morning, I drove to school, and I noticed that all the trees along the highway were encompassed in rustling gold.

A few weeks later, when Jonathan and I competed at sectionals, we got third place. We would qualify for the national championships.

Some things were falling into place.

18

Kiss and Cry

Exactly one year after leaving Arizona, I attended my first national championships.

Boston was the coldest place I'd ever been. Even colder than Colorado. A freezing wind forced my eyes shut as I stepped out the doors at Logan Airport. My lashes stuck together. I rushed into an Uber and slammed the door shut. As I slid into the back seat, I took a dramatic, teeth-chattering inhale.

"Where are you from?" the driver asked.

"Colorado," I answered, without thinking. "Well . . . originally Arizona," I added.

The driver laughed. "It doesn't snow like this in Arizona," he said.

"Yeah, I'm learning to dress warm," I said.

I had a good feeling about Boston, in spite of its harshness. As we drove past the city's old redbrick buildings, I marveled at the architecture. The streets divulged speckled patches of history. The people walked along the sidewalks with a kind of tension. Everyone seemed to be up to something urgent, and their bustling bodies offered a unique kind of comfort. Even after searching for a sense of home in two different states, I still mostly believed that I belonged best in places I wasn't from yet.

I took pictures out of the car's back window. I wanted to remember this exact moment. Ice dancing had taken me to one of the big East Coast cities of my dreams. It had taken me to my first national championships. It had brought me to what felt like a pinnacle. *This is what it's like when dreams come true,* I thought as we pulled up to the hotel.

Inside the lobby, a celebration materialized.

Red, white, and blue balloons marked the desk where competitors flocked to check in. Friends who lived on opposite sides of the county darted into one another's arms. Dozens of figure-skating icons could be found wandering through the hallways. After grabbing the keys to my room, I happened to step into the same elevator as an Olympic gold medalist, and I held my breath because I could hardly believe I was sharing the same air. The distance between me and the people I admired was narrowing right before my eyes.

The first official practice took place the following day. The ice was springy, and it projected a mighty cracking sound beneath my skates. It felt like skating in its purest form—like how I imagine the very first ice-skaters felt, with a frozen lake beneath their bodies and a glorious invention strapped to their feet. I barely noticed the judges who sat around watching us. I forced myself to absorb the memory of the glide and the echo.

At the novice level, the first part of the competition was composed of compulsory dances, and all skaters had to perform a waltz and a tango. Jonathan and I knew the compulsory dances were not our strength as a team, but we performed the best we could, and we focused our attention on the second part of the competition: the free dance. The free dance offered a chance to show more personality. Skaters could skate to any music they wanted. The program could be filled with all sorts of unique elements and dance styles—it was the perfect opportunity to tell a story on the ice. Jonathan and I had chosen to skate to a jazzy piece of music from the movie *The Godfather.*

The morning of the free dance, I was surprised when I woke up to the familiar sensation of butterflies. Everything had been so beautiful and new, I almost forgot to feel nervous.

To fight off the adrenaline rush, I distracted myself with getting ready. My mom had arrived in Boston a few days after me, and she helped with the process where she could, digging through my makeup bag to find the perfect shade of red lipstick, bobby-pinning the stray pieces of hair that I couldn't reach, and steaming the red satin of my dress. I liked being around my mom again. I liked having her there to help me. Since moving to Colorado, I got to see her in person only a few times a year, and I had a heightened appreciation of her company. She always offered a calming voice and a grounding smile.

When I was finally done, she stared at me for a long time.

"You look beautiful," she said. There was something a little bit sad in her voice.

Over the years, my mom had watched my body wax and wane. She didn't know how much time I had spent pinching my hips in the bathroom mirror, but she knew there was a hollowness in me. She could tell by the way my voice wavered when we spoke over the phone. When she first arrived in Boston, she seemed relieved to notice color in my cheeks.

"Thanks, Mom," I said. With my chest held up and my makeup done, I *felt* beautiful. I felt prepared to step in front of the crowd.

I gave my mom a hug, and we made our way to the arena.

***

In figure skating, the area where competitors wait to receive their scores is called the *kiss and cry.* It's usually just a fancy bench placed next to the boards of the rink. There are always a few boxes of tissues on hand and several cameras pointed toward the skaters.

There is drama in the name: *kiss and cry.*

Skating is a sport where hundreds of hours of hard work culminate in a pair of very short performances. The ice is slippery. Everyone wants to win. Emotions run high. The idea behind the kiss and cry is that if things go well, a celebratory kiss might occur, and if things go poorly, tears can be expected.

But here's the thing: Dramatic displays of emotion are *not* actually encouraged inside the kiss and cry. Almost every coach I've ever worked with has told me to save my true emotions for when I'm back at my own hotel room.

Don't show any weakness, they all said.

***

When my free dance ended, I sat in the kiss and cry, and I smiled when our scores were announced.

Jonathan and I ended up in tenth place out of a field of twelve teams. Jonathan was genuinely happy. My coaches were genuinely happy. It was a huge accomplishment just to compete at the event, and everyone seemed to be happy except for me.

I had wanted more.

Maybe it was in my nature to feel unfulfilled. Maybe I was a girl with too many feelings—too many disorderly, impolite, uncomfortable feelings—but I just wasn't content. I went back to the locker room, and I changed out of my costume, and I stepped into a bathroom stall, and I bit my lip to keep from crying. I felt guilty for not acting more grateful. It was my first national championships, after all, but I was impatient. I was hungry. I wanted to be one of the teams on the podium. I wanted to win, and it was the only kind of wanting I couldn't hold myself back from.

I took a deep breath and stepped out of the stall. I fixed my makeup in the mirror. I walked out of the locker room smiling.

Don't show any weakness.

I stayed in Boston for the rest of the week to watch the senior events (the highest level of competition). It was an

Olympic year, so the stakes were especially high. All the athletes would be bringing their best.

The arena was packed, and I disappeared into the stands. It was an uncanny experience, existing on the other side of the boards instead of lacing up my skates. Although I wasn't taking the ice, my legs couldn't quite keep still. A rush of nerves quickened my heartbeat. Even as an audience member, I couldn't separate myself from the thrill of the occasion.

The senior free dance event was held on a Saturday evening. A couple of days earlier, the rhythm dance had taken place. Instead of compulsory dances, skaters at the senior level performed their own take on a ballroom quick-step, and every team had shown sparkle and magnetism. The top-ranking teams would skate in the final warm-up group for the free dance.

When the final group of skaters took to the ice, a breeze blew through the stands. The teams were so fast. They circled like elegant, glittering racehorses. We could feel their power from yards away.

One team caught my eye: a tall blond girl with cascading curls and an even taller boy dressed in black and gray.

When the warm-up ended, an announcer boomed their names: "Please welcome to the ice Madison Hubbell and Zachary Donohue."

The whole crowd hushed to a ribbon-thin silence.

I had seen the pair on TV before, but something about their movement resonated differently up close. In real life, I could grasp the full magnitude of their presence. The program began with the silvery notes of a violin piece. Madison balanced effortlessly on one foot, then the other. She seemed to float and sink at will. I had never seen anyone with such command over a pair of blades.

Madison wasn't waiflike. She was luminous. Her legs were like mine—muscled and sturdy. Zach lifted her with no effort at all.

I held my breath for the entire four minutes of their program.

When the pair hit their final pose and the last violin note rang out, I realized I was crying. In the middle of a crowd.

All eyes were turned toward the center of the ice, where Madi and Zach were taking their bows. As is often the case when a truly magical performance ends, the audience seemed lost inside their own emotions.

Madi and Zach moved to the kiss and cry, and I don't remember what they did while they sat there—whenever I watch a really great program, I never notice what the competitors do in the kiss and cry—but I do remember letting myself completely surrender to the feeling they created. I didn't even wipe at my tears with my coat sleeves.

Something that had been shuttered inside me had flung itself agape.

When I returned to the lobby of the hotel, hundreds of competitors had gathered to give one another hugs and say goodbyes before catching flights home.

While I mingled with my peers, a friend sent me a text: *Do you want to attend your first-ever nationals after-party?*

I surprised myself by replying with an enthusiastic *Yes!!!!*

Within minutes, I found myself anxiously wandering the hotel hallways, trying to make sure I showed up at the right room.

Maybe this was a mistake, I thought, but before I could second-guess myself, I knocked on the door.

"Hey! Welcome!"

The voice belonged to a redheaded ice dancer named Joe, another skater who trained in Colorado Springs. He gave me a hug and then led me inside. Several teenagers and early-twenty-somethings were situated on the edges of two beds. The scene was milder than I'd expected. I assumed all skating parties were like the one I'd stumbled into when I first arrived in Colorado—all chaos and make-out and dancing.

Joe handed me a plastic Solo cup. Someone had brought a bottle of tequila and someone else had brought a bottle of soda, and everyone sipped on a crude mixture of both. I pretended that I was more familiar with alcohol than I actually was, and I tried not to make a pained face as I threw back a few generous sips.

Everyone was eating snacks. A box of donuts had been nearly emptied. Two bags of chips were lying in the trash. Every skater was celebrating with indulgence. We weren't trained in moderation. We had been waiting for this moment for months—the moment we could wash the hair spray from our hair and temporarily drop our diets and remove our lipstick smiles and let ourselves abandon the facade of purity. We were not machines built for our sport—we were humans, most of us young and desperate to experience different dimensions of ourselves.

I grabbed a donut and took a seat on one of the beds. My legs swung without touching the floor as I silently observed the rest of the room.

Joe walked over to sit next to me. Perhaps in an effort to counteract my obvious meekness, he struck up a conversation.

"Did you watch the senior dance event?"

"Yeah, of course," I said, my interest piqued.

"Okay, so which program was your favorite?" he asked.

"Easy," I said. "Madi and Zach made me cry." My voice came out a little boozy. I smiled. I was pleased by the new-found looseness of my vowels.

"Oh my god!" Joe said. "Me too!"

We looked at each other like we were both in on a

secret. We began quizzing each other on the results of past events: *Who is your favorite team of all time? Who has the most underrated programs? Who do you think is going to win the Olympics this year?*

I finished my donut and tipped back what was left of my drink.

Joe kept gushing about his favorite performances, and I nodded and listened. It was clear that he and I had similar obsessions. It was clear that we had both spent late nights memorizing step sequences on our bedroom floors and researching cha-chas and waltzes on the internet. We cared about skating with the same ravenous fury.

"Let's hang out again when we're back in Colorado Springs," I mused.

"That sounds like it would be fun," Joe replied.

When the party ended, I walked back to my own hotel room, but I paused to look out a window. My vision was the slightest bit tipsy. Boston's city lights hovered like fireflies caught inside a jar.

I noticed the outline of my own reflection in the window, and my reflection looked back without distorting itself—even after the donut, and the tequila, and the disappointing results of the competition.

It had taken longer than I had expected, but moving to Colorado *had* changed me into a new person. Maybe not in exactly the ways I had expected, but I was not the same girl I had been a year earlier. I stood a little taller than before. I wore heavier coats. I could cry without cringing—or at least *sometimes* I could cry without cringing. I could bring myself to attend a party. I could make new friends. I could walk through the hotel hallways with my heels clicking against the floor, and I actually wanted to spend more time with the person I was becoming.

After nationals, I ended my partnership with Jonathan. The results of the competition were the final breaking point. It had been a hard year training together, and our goals just didn't seem to quite match up. Plus, as my eating disorder continued to fade, I knew that I would always feel undue pressure to accommodate Jonathan's slight frame. I wanted to know what it felt like to stop being liquid—to stop constantly catering to the shape of another.

Jonathan and I went our separate ways, and I moved back home to Arizona while I searched for a new partner.

Jason and Britney moved out of the town house too. Our worlds were altering themselves all at once. Jason had earned a spot on the Olympic team, and when he returned from the games, he moved into the Olympic Training Center. Britney left for Canada to skate up north for several months. I planned to stay with my family while I searched for a new boy to skate with. My coaches in Arizona agreed to help me find potential partners.

When I returned home, the desert landscape appeared different. The cacti that had once appeared commonplace seemed novel and sacred. The heat felt more potent. I took on the role of a tourist, snapping pictures of sunsets with my phone. Deep down, I think I knew I wouldn't be staying for long.

I had my sights set on new goals. I scheduled a handful of tryouts and threw myself back into the partner-searching process.

On Valentine's Day, I went out to lunch with some old skating friends. While they whispered about potential Valentine's kisses, I got a text. I looked down at my phone, and my face instantly blushed.

"Is it a boy?" one girl asked with a mischievous scrunch at the corner of her eyes.

"Well . . . yeah," I replied. "But it's not what you think. . . ."

"Come on, just tell us!" they all insisted.

"It's a boy named Joe," I said. "He wants to be my new skating partner!"

"Well, maybe he can be a romantic partner too!" someone joked.

"No—it's not like that," I insisted. "Joe is gay. But you don't understand—this is so much better than a boyfriend."

And I believed what I said. My heart swelled because Joe's text meant that my dreams weren't over. I would head back to Colorado Springs to try out with Joe. My wild goals would get a second chance.

Spoiler: The tryout went well. Joe Johnson and I quickly became partners and best friends. To this day, we still celebrate being one another's favorite platonic Valentines.

19

Like Moth's Wings

After Joe and I teamed up, we began practicing right away.

Despite having been acquaintances for a while, we found ourselves struck by a sudden shyness. I circled the rink, keeping to myself. He glanced over every few minutes, like a timid house cat. A full hour passed as we stroked across the empty arena by ourselves.

"You know you're supposed to skate *with* each other, right?" our coach said when she finally intervened. We had been too nervous to approach one another, and we almost let the entire first day of training pass without even managing to hold hands.

I tried to laugh off the awkwardness. Sweat pooled

in my palm as I reached for Joe. We made a sheepish attempt to circle the rink with our hands clutched together. I wish I could say that when we finally connected, everything clicked and all the makings of a perfect partnership fell into place, but that isn't what happened. Our bodies didn't know one another yet. We were clumsy and uncoordinated. When I tried to go left, Joe chose to go right. We stumbled through the rest of the practice, wrong-footed and knock-kneed.

The next day wasn't much better.

I accidentally kicked Joe in the shin while we skated through a basic pattern together. I lost my breath as I tried to keep up with his unyielding speed. Our coach looked at me as if I was a baby calf trying to use its legs for the first time.

I had imagined skating with Joe from the moment I saw him training on the ice during my very first practice in Colorado Springs. I'd watched him dance a tango with his partner at the time: a beautiful blond skater with strong, sharp movements. Joe held her with confidence, and he framed her like art. *I wish that was me,* I thought. Maybe I should have felt a kick of guilt for wanting Joe—for wanting a partner who already belonged to someone—but I didn't think Joe would ever actually skate with me. I didn't think there was any real potential in my private fantasy.

Except, as fate would have it, my private fantasy had come true. Joe and his beautiful blond partner split up just after nationals—the same time that I ended things with Jonathan. (Joe and his partner were mismatched in terms of height, and they had a rough final season together.) Teaming up seemed like the natural next step for us both: We were the perfect sizes for one another, we were already casual friends, and—most important—we were both known to skate with a similar playful style that stuck out amid a field of other serious, sensual skaters.

The partnership *seemed* perfect, but during those first practices, as our coach stared me down with her critical gaze, I was beginning to question our pairing.

When Joe and I had agreed to partner up, we decided to train with his coaching team. Joe had experienced quite a bit of success under their direction, and I thought his coaches might be able to help mold us into an even more elite team. One coach in particular had a reputation for seriousness. Even before I started training with her, just being in her presence made me anxious, but I was willing to ignore my fears so I could give my partnership with Joe the best shot at fulfilling its potential. Right from the start, I felt like I had to constantly prove myself. Joe's coach knew that he was a strong, dedicated skater, but she didn't know much about me yet. I stepped into the rink every day hoping she wouldn't change her mind about me—hoping she wouldn't tell Joe that he was better off skating with someone else.

Despite my initial nervousness and the residual scab

on Joe's shin from my missteps, by the third day of practice, Joe and I began to settle into a more comfortable friendship.

That day, Joe turned on a warm-up playlist full of guitar-plucking indie songs—the kind of stuff you'd hear at a cool underground coffee shop—and I realized we had something else in common. The playlist was right up my alley. When I told Joe that I liked his taste in music, he lit up. For the rest of practice, he traded the names of his favorite folk singers for the names of my favorite alternative-rock albums. I left practice feeling like we had accomplished something—even if our skating still hadn't quite clicked yet.

Over the course of the next couple of weeks, we made dozens of playlists. I kept my headphones in at all hours, listening to Joe's recommendations. Joe showed up every morning with new finds. We texted constantly, gushing over our favorite musical gems: *Have you heard this song by the Fleet Foxes? You'd love the Paper Kites. Have you heard this one by Bleachers? You need to listen to more of Arctic Monkeys.* We had found a thread to connect us, and it became a bit of a game to keep surprising one another with fresh, exciting sounds.

One morning, I got to the rink early, excited to turn on another carefully composed playlist. It started with a song that had notes so sweet, they twinkled and blinked. The singer belted lyrics in an androgynous voice to a backdrop of joy and synth. It was a song called "Moth's Wings."

"I love this," Joe said. "Who is it?"

I felt my dimples forming, appearing as a result of my pride.

"This is Passion Pit. They're one of my favorite bands."

Over the next few days, Joe added some Passion Pit songs to his own playlists. He even found a few of their songs that I had never heard before. For some reason, this seemed like a sign—a good one.

Despite our budding friendship and our newfound common interest, the skating aspect of practices remained grueling and repetitive. There was a lot of pressure to do well at our first competition, which was set to take place in about four months. We both had only one more year to be eligible for international events at the junior level, and we thought this might be our only chance to skate together for Team USA. I felt like I had so much to prove. When the pressure seemed to be too much to bear, I lost myself in the beats of our background music; I pretended—as I had so many other times—that the long hours could montage together like a movie scene.

On the ice, Joe and I worked on elements I had never been able to attempt before: a lift where I hovered impossibly above his shoulders, a spin where I arched back into his arms like we could have been in love. Joe was stronger than my previous partner. He carried me with ease, and for the first time in a while, I didn't feel like I needed to be weightless.

But Joe's strength also took some adjusting to. The boundaries between Joe's body and my own were slight and delicate, like dotted lines. We needed more practice to learn how to manage the space between ourselves. When we spun together, the force of his arms pulled aggressively against my center, and I had to hold my breath to ignore the pain. I didn't want to seem weak, so for a long time, I didn't tell Joe or my new coach that I was hurting.

Then one day, something in our skating felt especially off. Our rhythms weren't in sync. Our bodies moved to different beats. We tried to work through the mistakes and force our skates to stay in motion, but we only made things worse. Joe pulled me into a spin, and we began turning together at a dizzying rate. His arms hugged my sides, wrapping around to my back. I arched—chest skyward— my limbs blooming and ribboning out from my spine. All at once, I felt a snap.

"I'm sorry. It's just . . . this position . . . it's really hurting me," I confessed.

Joe looked at me, concerned. Our coach looked at me, disappointed.

I instantly regretted admitting to the pain.

Our coach suggested that maybe I needed to add

more core exercises to my workout routine. I already had a pretty strong core, but I nodded. Maybe I wasn't quite strong enough to skate with Joe yet. I held planks in the gym that afternoon. And the next day. And the next day. After a couple of weeks, the pain didn't seem to get any better, but we didn't have time to slow down our training. Every practice brought us one day closer to our first competition. I learned to clench my jaw during spins in order to ignore the unrelenting pressure of Joe's pull.

When we were about two months out from the big event, I brought up the discomfort again during a lesson— more urgently this time—and my coach suggested *again* that the pain was probably a result of my lack of strength.

"Joe is going to spin with more force than your old partner did. You're going to have to get used to it," she said.

I swallowed the choking feeling of my unwanted disappointment. I knew crying would only make me seem more vulnerable. *Don't show any weakness,* I reminded myself. Joe looked at me sympathetically, but he didn't know how to help. Shame swelled in my stomach. I had considered myself tough, but for some reason, I wasn't able to handle any of the new elements with Joe. I had entered our partnership with so much hope, but I was beginning to question my abilities. Maybe I wasn't good enough. Maybe the tears I tried to argue back into my eyes were just another indication that I wasn't cut out for this partnership.

I went home from practice feeling defeated. That afternoon, I held planks while doing homework and watching TV.

Getting ready for bed that night, I put on one of the playlists Joe and I had built together. The stream of songs had the perfect balance of quiet and loud, the perfect combination of melody and beat. If only we collaborated as well on the ice as we did with our music tastes.

When I tried to fall asleep, I found that lying down was too painful. I attempted to create a makeshift pillow cloud around my torso to soothe the ache, but I couldn't get comfortable. Taking a quick breath caused my back to seize. I could no longer avoid my body the way I had always tried to. I couldn't starve off this kind of pain. In the mess of pillows and hurt, I resented the fact that I was so fragile.

The next day, my rib gave way entirely. Joe felt it pop underneath his hand. I knew because he immediately let go of me.

"Oh god . . . are you okay?" he asked. He turned to look at me and saw that I was doubled over, gripping the boards of the rink.

"Yeah . . . I think so. Just give me a second," I said. I attempted to catch my breath between words. "Actually, do you mind if I get off the ice for a few minutes? I think I need a break."

"Yeah, of course. Do you need to go to the doctor?"

"Um. I don't think so. . . . I'll be fine. . . ."

We sat at the bottom of the bleachers and unlaced our skates. Our coach walked over.

"I think I'm okay," I said before she had a chance to ask any questions.

"Maybe you should call it a day. I don't think your rib could be broken just from spinning, but you should probably get it checked out just in case," she said.

My face flushed with embarrassment. I hated the fact that I had gotten hurt *just from spinning.* The way her words came out with the slightest hint of skepticism made me question if I was really hurt. Maybe I was too sensitive. Maybe I was overreacting.

Joe drove me to the doctor, and I waited inside a cold room wearing only a paper gown. A nurse asked me to rate my pain on a scale of one to ten.

I lied.

"Three. Maybe a four," I said.

I had secretly hoped the nurse would interrupt me and tell me to choose a higher number. Even inside the walls of the doctor's office, I worried about coming across as over-dramatic. I wanted someone to tell me it was okay to feel my pain at a seven or an eight. Instead, the nurse just nodded and guided me toward another exam room.

There, an X-ray tech walked me to a machine and instructed me to place a little metal sticker over the area where I'd felt the snap. As I ran my hands over my skin to feel for the right spot, I was reminded of all the times, not long before, when I had touched my ribs the very same way to make sure I was thin enough. This time, I slid my fingers across my bones with great care. For the first time in my life, I felt thankful for the layer of protection between my skeleton and the world.

The X-ray tech moved me through a series of poses, trying to get a good picture of my ribs. I attempted to read her expression while she looked at the images, but she remained inscrutable, oblivious to my questioning gaze. She walked me back to the exam room without giving away any of my results.

I felt strangely validated when the doctor returned with the news.

"You have a fracture on your eleventh rib." She gestured to a line in my X-rays, which had been pulled up on a computer. "It's not displaced, and it won't require surgery, but you're going to have to take it easy for a while."

It felt like the doctor had finally given me permission to truly acknowledge the ache I had been sensing for weeks. I took in a heavy breath and winced at everything I could feel. Lying on the exam table, bashful in my paper gown, I turned to Joe. I tried to make my expression say, *See? I knew I wasn't overreacting!*

Joe looked back with kindness, as if his expression was trying to say, *I believed you all along.*

But the news meant it would be even harder for us to

be ready in time for our first competition. We were both a bit discouraged. I had to stay completely off the ice for a week, and when I returned, we weren't allowed to work on any spins or lifts.

The day that I came back to practice, my whole being was dampened with an exceptional sense of solemnity. I thought my chances of making Team USA had been crushed. I wondered if there was even a point to showing up at the rink again.

Perhaps in an effort to cheer me up, Joe cued a playlist of songs we had curated together. The twinkling notes and falsetto vocals of "Moth's Wings" began to play. It made me feel a little better. Joe took my hand, and we crisscrossed our blades over the ice.

"I think this might be my favorite song," Joe and I both said—not quite in perfect unison, but almost.

"You know . . . Passion Pit is playing a concert in Denver next month. It'll be on a Tuesday night. If we go, we'll be exhausted at practice the next day, but"—I paused to let my voice drag out—"it might still be worth it just to hear this song live."

I tried to read Joe's expression. I almost never acted on impulse. I've always had a hard time staying awake past ten, especially on weeknights, but I was overtaken by a strange wave of recklessness. I wanted to feel young and careless. I wanted to forget that I was hurt. Something told me to let go of my responsibilities, just for a moment.

"I think we should do it," Joe said. We bought our tickets that night.

As we counted down the days to the concert, my rib steadily sealed itself. Some nights I held my hand softly over my side and imagined the cells regenerating beneath my skin, and I marveled at how resilient my body could be.

While I was recovering, Joe held me like a cloud, like a whisper. He was terrified of hurting me again. This new, softer technique took a bit of practice to master. With Joe's delicate grip, and with my gentle lean against his arms, we weren't initially able to spin as fast as we once could, and we struggled to keep our balance centered, but eventually our elements began to work. In fact, they began to work better than ever. We were starting to look like actual dancers—not just stumbling calves.

By the time the concert rolled around, I was no longer in much pain.

As Joe drove us away from our city up the stretch of land that separates Colorado Springs from Denver, a thunderstorm rolled over downtown. Every couple of minutes, lightning struck some lucky piece of earth, and the brightness was so bold that it could be felt even from inside the venue.

Behind a haze of smoke and spotlights, Passion Pit took the stage. Joe and I shuffled our way to the middle of the audience, bouncing and bobbing alongside a mass of sweaty, rain-soaked bodies. The band played loud enough that we all forgot about the storm. We forgot about our regular lives and our everyday problems—we let ourselves take a few moments to think of nothing except the saccharine beats and the drippy lyrics. We belted until we couldn't find our breath. The electricity seemed to infect us for hours, and just when the buzz felt like it might begin to dim, the band played the first twinkling notes of "Moth's Wings." We listened to the tender, breathy buildup. We anticipated the flood of the chorus. Our heartbeats stirred with the sweetness of the melody, and we let the moment be fragile and fleeting as a blink.

Joe and I stayed until the crowds were forced to file back into the storm and the cars were sent off to drive home. It was nearly two in the morning. We knew that by the time we made the journey to our empty beds, we would get only about an hour of sleep—we had to be at practice before the sun was up—but we didn't mind.

When we got to the rink, Joe played the soundtrack from the night before. A chorus of perfect notes echoed through the rink's speakers. We smiled at one another— each of us holding our small secret inside the bags under our eyes. I think that was the moment we knew our partnership would work out. It had become official during the stretched-out moments of our sleepless night: We were in this together. We were on the same team.

Joe took me by the hand and tossed me into a spin. He then reached around my lower back, and I arched into

20

First and Second Kisses

During my first year of skating with Joe, I decided to take a step away from the world of academics. Unlike a lot of skaters I knew, who were homeschooled throughout large portions of their careers, I attended high school full-time. (My parents were pretty adamant about the importance of education, which is something I never fully appreciated until I got older.) I had always been a really good student, but sometimes I struggled to find a balance between my grades and my competitions. I got panic attacks before big tests. I stayed up entire nights completing essays because I couldn't bring myself to sleep until they were done. When high school ended, I wanted to focus most of my energy on my Olympic aspirations, and my parents agreed to let me take a break.

So I did what a lot of teenagers do: I took a gap year.

Without the constant burden of homework, my days quickly grew busy with other tasks. I boosted my off-ice training routine—adding more dance classes and workouts to my schedule—and I took on a part-time job at a day care to help cover some of my training costs. Looking after children still didn't come naturally to me, but the job offered flexible hours, and I was slowly getting the hang of caring for myself and others.

At the outset of the season, my potential growth seemed borderless. With a new partner, a new coaching team, and a new schedule, I was sure that international competitions and gold medals were just beyond my sight lines.

But despite the optimism that I entered the season with, my partnership with Joe kept toppling into major bumps. When my broken rib healed, I suffered another injury, which would devastate our prospects for the summer competitions. At practice one day, Joe and I collided in a forceful and violent instant. I buckled to the ice, clutching my leg. As I peeled my fingers away from my tights, blood laced its way to the floor in slow beads. I looked down to see a horrifying set of Jackson Pollock drips against the ice. Joe's blade had sliced deep into one of my knees.

When we arrived at an urgent care, a nurse rushed me

into a room. The doctor informed me that I had been cut all the way down to my bone. Joe held my hand while the doctor stitched the halves of my flesh back together.

I returned to practice the very next day because I didn't want my injury to be the reason we weren't named to Team USA. Perhaps someone should have stepped in. Maybe someone should have told me to rest, or told me that getting hurt wasn't my fault, or told me that I would have a career full of so many other chances—but nobody told me that, so I clenched my jaw, and I tried to continue as if my life wasn't being held together by sixteen tiny threads. Letting myself be soft was much easier said than done.

Of course, the injury deeply shook my confidence. Several months passed before I was able to skate with the same assuredness that I had possessed before getting hurt, and by the time my shakiness subsided, it was too late—Joe and I had already missed our chance to be named to Team USA for the season.

While I tried to overcome the emotional blow of losing out on our goals, I realized that I longed for the comforting distraction of school. I missed being around people who didn't want to talk about twizzles and curve lifts. I missed feeling like there was more to my life than the elusive desire to wear a red-white-and-blue jacket.

I missed building casual friendships and writing

research papers and nurturing unrequited crushes. *My god*, I missed having crushes. There is maybe nothing quite as blissfully distracting as daydreaming about love.

So as Joe and I headed into the senior ranks for our second season together, I ended my gap year and applied to take classes at the nearby university.

For a long time, I used to tell people I met in Colorado that I had my first kiss at the eighth-grade dance. I would make up a story about how there were fairy lights strung above the patio outside the school's administrative offices (there were). How I wore a hot pink dress that bunched at the bottom in a way that can only be described as *very 2008* (I did). How, under those fairy lights, I kissed a boy who flipped his hair out of his eyes before he leaned in (this part is obviously the lie). As you know, the truth is that the boy with the flippy hair didn't go to the dance with me or with anyone at all. I wasn't quite the feminist I became a few years later, and I didn't yet have the reckless abandon required to ask him. Instead, I went to the eighth-grade dance with a group with friends who were equally dis-illusioned by the spectacle of such an occasion without an awkward tuxedoed boy to share it with.

My first kiss actually came later. Much later.

I was a freshman in college.

A guy named Leo and I were nestled next to each other on his dorm-room floor. The party was hitting its crest, and his room was in a state of mild disarray—like a beach after the tide has rolled out. We dragged his comforter off the bed and propped up a couple of pillows behind our backs to create a sort of makeshift nest. A few empty pizza boxes had been pushed into a corner. The recycling bin overflowed with cans of Sprite and cheap beer. Leo lived in the honors dorm on campus, so alcohol and weed were especially prohibited, but some adventurous freshman had smuggled both into the party anyway. Leo slowly sipped on one of the beers. I was too nervous to drink at all that night, so I pretended to have vodka in my Solo cup, when in reality I was just drinking Sprite.

Leo and I had met a couple of months earlier. As a now-proud writer and queer woman, I'm a little ashamed to admit that the first time I set foot on my college campus, my academic pursuits felt secondary to my desire to finally kiss a boy. I had gone nearly twenty years without ever attaching myself to a boyfriend, and I was beginning to question my own capacity to draw affection. Could someone love me? Was I too anxious? Too emotional? Too hairy, and sweaty, and unsure of what to say?

I decided freshman orientation would be a good place to search for answers. Maybe someone in the crowd of new bodies would be able to finally break my streak of undesirability.

Inside a bustling auditorium, my eyes immediately spotted Leo because he was wearing the same dark-framed glasses as me, and he had on the kind of button-up shirt that said he liked local restaurants and vinyl records. I smiled at him from behind my eyelashes, in a way that I wanted to look flirty but probably just looked like I was mistaking him for someone I knew. Regardless, I somehow caught his attention, and he slipped next to me during the campus tour. When he asked me my name, my unlucky, frantic heart decided we were already basically dating.

While Leo and I wandered behind our overly enthusiastic tour guide, we swapped stories about the cities we were from, and we quietly slid past the students who were taking the get-to-know-each-other games way too seriously. We made our way through the campus's various buildings, familiarizing ourselves with the place that would be our new home. Our campus sat on a hill, and on that day, it felt especially close to the sky.

Orientation carried on, and we were eventually ushered into a computer lab to register for our first set of classes. When Leo noticed that I had an opening in my schedule, he suggested that I take the same public-speaking class as him. I agreed to his suggestion, which—in hindsight—I can admit was a completely reckless decision. I barely knew the guy, and suddenly I was signing up for a class constructed around one of my worst fears. But in that naive moment, desperation prevailed over a remarkable case of stage fright. I was determined to make Leo my first kiss, even if it meant forcing myself to give speeches every Wednesday.

On the first day of class, Leo saved me a seat, and I let my insides melt into a warm puddle. All through the class, he found excuses to brush my arms or poke my sides. Pink rose to the top of my cheeks and stayed there, like a fog waiting to greet the sunrise.

My dizzying affection almost distracted me enough to make me forget about the speeches.

Almost.

Each week I would sweat profusely on the way to the lecture hall, hyperventilating the words to my speeches under my breath, trying to body-spray away the she's-been-profusely-sweating smell in the seconds before I entered the room. Somehow Leo remained, if not romantically interested, at least a little intrigued by me.

When the lecture ended, we'd walk back to his dorm room together. I probably looked at his lips too often; he probably wondered why I was still so horrifically clumsy at the whole flirting charade. One time it rained, and he let me borrow his umbrella so I could stay dry while walking to my next class.

The following Friday night, he asked if I was busy, and even though I was supposed to be going to dinner with

Joe, I told Leo I'd be right over. (Joe didn't mind; he understood the monumental first-kiss potential that the night held. He was one of the few people who knew that my go-to first-kiss story was a lie.) By the time I got to Leo's building, a party had already begun to lose its inhibitions. His hallway buzzed. Stumbling freshmen fumbled at the beer pong table in the common area of his dorm, and after making small talk and mingling for a few minutes, Leo and I quietly snuck into the privacy of his room, where he suggested we watch something on Netflix—this wasn't a very original move, but I didn't mind. I wanted every overused plotline. I had waited so long to feel what it seemed like every other college freshman girl in the world had already felt before.

I let all my anticipation simmer and boil over.

After Leo pushed the pizza boxes aside and arranged his pillows on the floor, he turned on some comedy starring Seth Rogen. I don't remember what the movie was called, because I wasn't paying much attention to the screen at all. I was mostly thinking about the boy's hand on my leg—the way his touch made my body feel unfolded.

With a gentle smile, Leo took off his dark, wide glasses and brought his face to mine. I rolled toward him, and our lips met slowly and sweetly. He didn't taste like strawberries, which was what I had been expecting. Instead, he tasted a little like cologne and a little like alcohol, and mostly like another person's mouth—which is a taste that only really tastes like itself. Every once in a while, we opened our eyes to take a breath and giggle at one another.

"You good?" he asked.

"Yeah, I'm good," I said. I knew I was smiling too much when I replied. My dimples have always ruined my poker face.

"Are *you* good?" I asked back, trying to play it cool, trying not to let on that his kisses were my first.

"Yeah," he answered. I was endlessly relieved when his cheeks sank into dimples too.

Our mouths found one another again. The Seth Rogen movie kept streaming. Our bodies moved together in an unrestrained, magnetic way. We both became acutely aware of our parts: hips, necks, hands. My nerves felt awake—like I had never tested out my senses before. Like I was noticing that I had skin for the very first time. I remember thinking that kissing really did live up to all the hype.

Leo's roommate opened the door—and like anyone who has ever been walked in on, we jumped apart and tried to pretend that our bodies had never been pressed together. The roommate laughed and made a crude joke that wasn't worth remembering. A few other guys stormed the room and asked us to join in another round of beer pong. The party was clearly slowing down, but some determined sophomore playing DJ was convinced he could revive it.

I reluctantly joined the mingle of drunken students

until the music ran out and everyone finally returned to their respective rooms. Because I was living off campus and had to drive home, Leo offered to walk me to my car. When we got to the parking lot, I hoped he would kiss me again, but he didn't. Instead, he hugged me, and I thought my joints might all disconnect in his arms. I wanted nothing more than for him to keep holding me together.

During the drive home, I thought: *See? That was so fun! I had the best time! I must not be gay!* (These days, if you were to ask me to name the top five most queer things a person could think after kissing someone for the first time, *I had fun, I must not be gay* would definitely make the list, but I didn't know any better back then.)

I floated down the highway and chose to think about the exact curve that connected Leo's shoulder to his biceps—how smooth it was and how strong. The traffic lights seemed to blink brighter than normal. I moved leisurely. I realized I liked the feeling of being liked by someone.

Unfortunately, the feeling didn't last.

Leo and I kept walking to and from class together, but after a couple of weeks—and without any hint of a reason—his interest began to fade. I can only speculate about what might have happened: Maybe he met a prettier girl in a different class; maybe my eagerness put him off; maybe he was just another very attractive boy with a short attention span.

It didn't make any sense, but the more Leo pulled away, the more desperately I wanted to pull him close. He stopped poking my sides during lectures, but I kept letting him borrow my notes. One day in class, he opened a dating app and swiped through the pictures of other girls right in front of me, but I acted like I didn't notice or care. I kept telling myself to play things cool. I should have moved on, but Leo continued texting me just often enough to make me think there was still hope for something to reignite between us. I tried to invite him to another party one weekend, but he claimed he already had other plans. I imagined he was sipping a beer on his dorm-room floor, watching the same Seth Rogen movie but kissing a different girl. I tried not to be upset. He wasn't even my boyfriend. We had just flirted off and on for a few months. He was just someone who wanted me and then didn't.

I felt dumb for all the time I'd spent daydreaming about him.

For a while, I allowed our strange pseudo-relationship to persist (and maybe I would have let it persist even longer), but I stopped seeing Leo when the semester ended, and it got a lot easier to distract myself from missing his affection.

On the bright side, I entered the next semester much better at public speaking.

In the spring, I found myself in the vicinity of several other boys who liked me in an unattached, unflinching way. Some of them were classmates who were taken aback by the way I had begun to talk during class—sparingly, but with a noticeable boost in confidence. Some of them were guys I had swiped through on dating apps. Some of them were just tipsy bodies at various parties. They all told me I had nice eyes.

I'm not sure exactly what changed. Maybe boys began to crush on me because I had learned to force a slight sway in my hips when I walked. Maybe it was because I had started looking at guys directly—almost challengingly—when they spoke to me. Maybe it was just the fact that I had gained a little more belief in myself.

But a small part of my mind couldn't help but believe that Leo's lukewarm affection had set off a chain reaction. I didn't give myself enough credit. I ascribed my sudden likability to the interest of one stupid boy, and when he disappeared, I worried the spell would wear off. I treated attention the same way desert plants treat water—I hoarded it because I was afraid of another drought.

Amidst my fear of droughts, I met a guy I'll call Tyler.

We had a class together, and in the early weeks of the semester, I had let him borrow one of my books. He spoke with bold, enunciated words, and he liked movies I had never heard of. When he called them *films*, I didn't detect his pretension. We chatted a few times in the hallways. At some point, he got my phone number. I was slightly interested in him, and he was slightly interested in me, and we orbited each other until one night when he asked me if I wanted to grab dinner at a restaurant near campus. I was already a little sad and a little bored that night, so I agreed. I had been spending a lot of time trying to make plans for my birthday, but Joe was going to be out of town, and Britney was still living in Canada, and Jason was going to be busy at a skating event. I had other casual friends, but I wasn't sure if I could work up the nerve to ask them to spend my birthday with me. When Tyler offered to take me out, I was relieved to be given a bit of a distraction.

We ate dinner outside. We sat with a group of his friends who had coalesced around a table. The experience reminded me of high school, which made me recoil. I subconsciously folded my arms over my torso and stared at my shoes. While we ate, Tyler cracked a few jokes that genuinely made me laugh. I forced awkward conversation with some of his friends, but the whole time I felt the strange sensation of being paraded around and shown off—like a pretty foreign bird. It was as if Tyler had brought me only to flaunt his own dating success: *Look at me. Look at the girl who is hanging out with me.* And for a split second, I missed feeling like someone unnoticeable.

When dinner ended, Tyler invited me back to his dorm, and I couldn't come up with a good excuse to decline, so I didn't. The date wasn't going particularly well, but it also wasn't going particularly poorly, so I resolved to stick it out in case the awkwardness was just nerves. We walked back to his dorm slowly. The sun was setting, and the disappearing light left a glowy gold outline along the mountains. I can't recall anything we talked about as we walked. I wasn't paying very close attention to our conversation—I was still contemplating the fact that birthdays are always either really happy or really sad, and there's never an in-between. I debated telling Tyler about my revelation, but it felt like too personal a thought for first-date dialogue. Tyler kept talking, and I nodded at the appropriate moments, and I kept quietly wondering about all the people who had ever bought themselves their own birthday cakes.

I like to think my body language was beginning to show some feelings of reservation, but maybe it wasn't.

When we got to Tyler's dorm, Tyler grabbed me and pressed his lips to mine. It happened that quickly: my second kiss. It was an uncoordinated sort of kiss. A few moments passed before I responded at all. Then I cautiously let my lips move with his. There was no buildup. No chance to form anticipation. Just the taste of another mouth: sudden and harsh.

This kiss was different from the one on Leo's floor. Leo had been slower and more tender. His hands had inched their way to my waist. Tyler's hands didn't question.

I pulled away.

"I'd like to keep this fairly PG, if that's okay?" I said.

"Sure," he replied, and then he kissed me again. I felt him pulling at the edges of my sweater, and I gently moved his hands to my hips.

"We don't have to do anything, but can I at least take off your shirt?" he asked. His eyes were squeezed shut, more forcefully than necessary. His palms found their way to the bottom of my sweater again. He opened his eyes and backed away for a breath.

"I mean . . . sure . . . I guess," I said. I could have said no, but Tyler smelled nice, and I could feel the crackling of my skin like the ground in the desert, and I did not know how to reject something that I was so scared of living without, and I did not know how to draw boundaries around a body that was so used to being pushed beyond its limits.

Tyler threw my sweater on the floor, and I wished he hadn't. It looked wrong next to the clutter of books and sweatshirts covering his carpet. I felt naked in my bra and jeans. *It's okay,* I told myself. *You've been more naked at public pools.* He took off his own shirt. His torso was smooth and strong and plain. I put a hand to his chest, and we kissed again, and I didn't say anything. I tried to move my lips in ways that I hoped would soften Tyler's mouth. This worked with varying degrees of success.

Eventually, I told Tyler I had to use the bathroom. I tried not to notice my body in his mirror, but I have never been very good at avoiding my reflection. My skin looked colorless. My cheeks looked puffy. The bathroom was running dangerously low on both toilet paper and soap. I remember standing alone at his sink, realizing for the first time that Tyler didn't have a roommate and thinking about how unusual that was. I wondered how he had managed to arrange his solo living quarters at a school that was spilling over with so many students.

When I returned, we positioned ourselves on his bed. He opened his laptop to play an episode of a show we both liked. It was a popular crime drama, and watching it together somehow felt too serious for the occasion. Tyler put an arm around my shoulders, and its weight sank into my neck. Neither of us seemed comfortable. He kept leaning over to kiss me. I kept reminding myself that I had chosen to be there. Our bodies were awkward, refusing to yawn into one another. I tried to stare out his window, but it was covered by dark curtains, so I started at those instead.

"What are you thinking about?" he asked, smirking slightly. I inflated with irrational annoyance. I had never liked that question, and I especially didn't like the way Tyler asked it. He probably didn't mean to, but he sounded entitled to the thoughts that were occurring in the privacy of my own head. I didn't want to give him the real answers: *I'm thinking about how I'm probably going to have to buy my own birthday cake in a few days. I'm thinking about how I wish I could make up a convincing excuse to leave your room. I'm thinking about how I wish you had a roommate to*

interrupt us. I'm thinking about how I wish your window was
open right now. . . .

"I don't know . . . I'm not really thinking about anything," I said.

"I'm thinking about how beautiful you are," he said.

My annoyance flipped the switch to a surprising rage.
I felt the brief, cold desire to send my fist into his wall.
Mostly, I was angry at myself for feeling attracted to Tyler,
but I was also angry at him for throwing my sweater on the
floor, and for holding my body too tightly, and for calling
me beautiful in a way that felt unearned. I was angry at
the way our conversations sounded like we were reading
from a bad script. I was angry at myself all over again because I still couldn't bring myself to leave. I began to reply
to Tyler's sentences with one-word answers.

Thanks. Okay. Sure.

He took my quiet answers as an opportunity to move
his mouth back to mine. His hands grabbed at my body
with strength—too heavy, too assured. I didn't respond. I
wasn't exactly scared, but I wished the window was open
and someone would walk by and cause an interruption. I
needed a little more air. I could feel Tyler's longing fill the
room. I was so distanced from my own desire, I couldn't
remember what wanting felt like.

At various low moments of my eating disorder, I was
so afraid to eat that I would have sworn I stopped feeling

hunger. Of course, I still was hungry, but I couldn't recognize the feeling anymore. The point is that kissing Tyler was not the first time my body had rendered itself incapable of knowing what it needed. The point is that I spent years mixing up a great deal of terror into almost all my cravings. The point is that almost every woman I know has seen desire and fear bleed into the same cloth.

Tyler did not stop moving closer to me. I didn't tell him to stop.

My body curled inward slightly—but I should have known better. The act of shrinking my body had never been able to substitute for words that were difficult for me to say aloud.

Tyler's hands searched for the place where my jeans met my waist, and they lingered there as if testing what they could get away with. His mouth bit against the skin surrounding my bra straps. I stopped breathing, but I kept kissing him back. I regret it, but I kept kissing him back. He drew his palm along the insides of my thighs. I'm not sure how much time passed—it could have been seconds, but it felt so much longer—before he began fiddling around the zipper of my jeans. My hand slowly, gently moved his away.

"It's getting late. I have to go."

"Ah, come on. Where do you have to be?"

"I told my roommate I'd be home. She's probably wondering where I am."

"You could stay here if you want."

"No, my roommate will be worried."

"Okay. Let me walk you to your car."

"You really don't have to."

"No. I will."

The walk to my car was rushed. My feet attempted to keep a pace faster than Tyler's, even though his legs were much longer than mine and his stride was naturally much quicker. When we got to my car, Tyler grabbed me and kissed me again. This time, I didn't kiss him back at all.

When I got home, it was just past midnight. I immediately took a shower and tried to wash away my skin. Steam drifted toward the ceiling, and I imagined myself evaporating the same way the water did. When I left the shower, I was relieved that the mirror had fogged over. I didn't want to look at myself.

Tyler and I didn't really speak much after that. I told him I was uncomfortable with the way that our date had played out, and he apologized, and it seemed like he really meant it, and I told him not to worry about anything because I truly didn't want either of us to worry about anything, and then we stopped making eye contact during class.

A few days later, my birthday arrived, and I spent it alone. I never worked up the courage to ask some of my casual friends to spend the day with me. I knew things could have been worse, but I still spent a good portion of the day softly shower weeping. I didn't bother buying myself a cake.

When the semester ended, I asked Tyler to give back the book he had borrowed; it was a book I had really liked—a play called *Stop Kiss* that explored a delicate romantic relationship between two women before one of them faces a violent attack. Tyler admitted that he had only skimmed it. When he handed the paperback over, he pressed the covers together as if a secret was trying to escape from the pages. I could tell that something was wrong.

The book had been badly water-damaged. The cover was warped like old wood.

Tyler never apologized for damaging my book. He just handed it over and left.

For months, I wasn't sure what to make of our interactions. After the date, I tried to push him out of my mind. *Nothing really happened,* I told myself (those words were written over and over in my journal at the time), and even now, I half believe them. But one night, I picked up the paperback that I had lent to him, and I found myself restaining the book with my tears.

I think—like a lot of girls—I learned that there is a gray area of desire. I had wanted to go on the date with Tyler, I had wanted to kiss him, but I had also wanted it all to happen so differently. I didn't understand how to make it all happen differently.

The confusion made my world shift. I taught myself

to always have an excuse to leave a room. For a long time, I stopped letting men borrow my books. Classes carried on, and I kept showing up to dorm-room parties without completely knowing why. I kissed more lips that tasted like cologne, and I didn't always stop kissing when I wanted to stop kissing, but I kept trying to untangle my fears from my desires. Sometimes, I wondered if Tyler's world had changed too. Did he start to move slower? Is he a little more thoughtful with the books he borrows now?

I hope so. . . . I like to hope so.

When the end of the semester approached, I felt relieved to be getting away from campus. Summer arrived, and I read the waterlogged play about the two women who were once in love over and over.

21

All the Things
I've Kept from Myself

Amid the year of unprecedented kisses, I also took a bunch
of classes. While I wove in and out of crushes on boys, I
fell head over heels in love with school. (For the record,
I found the latter to be a much more productive form of
affection.)

I adored college. The entire experience was so different from high school. I didn't feel lonely when I sat alone
on campus. I wasn't embarrassed to care deeply about the
content of my textbooks. Instead, I often felt small in a
beautiful and important way. Like a blade of grass. Like a
honeybee.

I quickly claimed a large table in the library as my own.

It sat next to a huge window, and I studied there for hours on end, lost in the beams of sunlight that poured over the pages of my notes. I was sucked down a whirlpool of discovery. I wanted to take every single course the school offered. I wanted to major in every subject. I remember asking my counselor about the fine arts program and the political science program and the philosophy program. I think I finally chose the English department for a very simple reason: It meant I would get to spend more time at my cherished library window, flipping through gentle piles of books.

There was only one class that I dreaded attending: a literature class, required of all English majors, where students had to read John Milton's epic poem *Paradise Lost*. I was intimidated by the archaic language of the book, and I never felt confident in my abilities to wrestle with religious content, so I usually sat in the back of the room and watched the clock count the hours away.

To make matters worse, my professor was a stuffy man who refused to answer any student's questions. *Well, what do you all think?* he'd parrot back at us, gesturing his arms widely toward the ungracious sea of listeners.

Needless to say, I found myself resorting to SparkNotes and Wikipedia to complete most of my assignments. Through my lazy internet research, I learned that *Paradise Lost* was a retelling of the Genesis story: Adam. Eve. The infamous forbidden fruit . . .

I always got nervous when discussions of Christianity arose inside classrooms. I had memories from high school that left a residual tension in my body.

Years before, during a ninth-grade history class, I had silently observed while other students argued about whether or not gay people should be allowed to serve openly in the military. Maybe at another school, the debate would not have spiraled out of control, but Chandler was still a pretty conservative city, and the only time I ever heard LGBTQ+ people discussed in classrooms was when their rights were being questioned. The discussion rapidly branched off into other debates: Should on-campus Christian clubs be able to ban LGBTQ+ members? Should same-sex couples be allowed to legally marry? Is being gay morally wrong?

I tentatively raised my hand to participate. I was still sure that I was straight, but I felt a clawing urge to join the conversation. My classmates' words were getting so cruel. Tensions were mounting. I wanted to come to the defense of the LGBTQ+ community (this was my chance to be an ally!), but before the teacher could call on me, she nodded in the direction of another classmate's raised hand.

The classmate who spoke was a sweet-looking Christian girl. She had shiny braids and perfectly even skin. She stared me directly in the eyes while she spoke.

"The Bible describes marriage as between a man and

a woman. We shouldn't be changing the definition now. It has been this way since *Adam and Eve*."

My classmate smiled at the end of her sentence, but she let harshness seep into her voice. Her stare held in a way that made me believe she could see into my soul. I was sure she wanted to extract any queer desire that lay in the depths of my subconscious.

I rolled my eyes at her comments, but I put my raised hand back down.

I left the classroom feeling oddly shaken.

From that moment on, I dreaded when Adam and Eve dipped their way into classroom discussions—the conversation surrounding them never felt like a safe one for me. I always got too emotional. Too nervous. Too invested.

Despite the fact that I knew plenty of affirming Christians, I feared any and all classes that dealt with the Bible's original heterosexual couple.

Even with all my initial hesitancies, I made my way through the pages of *Paradise Lost* each week, and I found myself interested in the epic poem's story line: It was captivating, really. I took notes in the margins of my book while my professor talked about complicated literary theories. I was still too scared to ask any questions or participate much—but I grew to like the flamboyance of Satan.

The mysteriousness of God. The unsettling perfection of Adam. I had to admit, the Bible set Milton up with a charismatic cast of characters.

My favorite character of all was Eve.

When she first showed up in the story, her presence made me gasp. I sat in my back corner of the classroom while some more assured students read aloud. Their voices carried me into the tale.

In her first scene, Eve stares at her reflection in the pearly surface of a lake. A garden surrounds her—the landscape is full of lush trees and succulent flowers and a sky so vast and blue, its color drips onto the earth's skin. While Eve admires her reflection, she grazes the side of her hand against the surface of the lake, causing the entire image to shiver. Eve has crystalline eyes, and she cannot draw them away from her reflection. She cannot comprehend the beauty and foreignness of her own body.

Eve must think it is so strange to be alive.

Eventually, Adam appears, and Eve turns to him. She gazes upon his form, which is somehow both familiar and confusing. At first glance, Eve feels tempted to turn away from Adam. She wants to look back at the comfort of her own reflection, but she forces herself to stare at the man who is meant to be her partner and love.

Eve knows not to follow all her impulses. She knows she is supposed to adore only Adam, so she smiles at him.

She learns to hold her true desires back.

Although I was inside a classroom—far, far from the Garden of Eden—my leg twitched beneath my desk. I felt tempted to run to Eve, to tell her not to feel ashamed. I wanted to tell her to keep adoring her own reflection.

I could only take a breath and close the book that had been lying open on my desk.

"What do you all think?" my professor asked in his usual taunting voice.

Everyone else in class was quick to declare that Eve was too vain and too shallow—a woman motivated by ego and arrogance—but I felt defensive of her. I knew there were a thousand reasons to stare into a mirror that had nothing to do with self-obsession. Maybe Eve was just trying to make sense of her own existence. Maybe she was just trying to comprehend the absurdity of being carved from Adam's rib.

After class ended, I walked across campus toward the library. Luckily, my favorite table was empty. I sat facing the window, so light dripped across my face. Then I began taking selfies. I explored the oddness of my own reflection with a new kind of rebellious joy. It seemed like I was honoring Eve in the tiniest way.

In the days that followed, I spoke up a little more during class. I felt less afraid of the archaic language of *Paradise Lost*—Eve's problems did not seem so different from my own. I might not have understood complicated literary theory, but I understood what it was like to be a woman who was ashamed of the addictive relationship she had with her reflection.

A few weeks later, my class was assigned a large section of reading. Our professor told us that this section might be the most important part of the entire book: the Fall.

I situated myself in the library. I relished the opportunity to dive into the book without the critical comments from my professor and the confident assertions from my classmates.

Students circled the surrounding shelves and tables and chairs, but I hardly noticed their movements.

I opened my tattered copy of *Paradise Lost* and flipped through the pages, nearing the back cover. At first, I drudged through the demanding stanzas, making notes here and there, sometimes pausing to look up certain words, but after a few minutes, I found myself slipping back into the story—watching as if I was hidden behind the shadowy branches of a tree. While reading, I got lost in the story, experiencing the sights and sounds as if I had come to life in the garden myself.

Inside the garden, Adam and Eve both wake up to fevering rays of sunlight. Eve yawns and stretches her arms wide. The garden's foliage rustles in the breeze. A flock of birds flies overhead. The air smells sweet and citrusy.

Eve—in a burst of impulsive curiosity—asks Adam if she can work in the garden on her own for the day. She fidgets, tucking a stray curl behind her ear. She is nervous to hear her lover's response.

Adam agrees to let Eve venture off, but not without some hesitation. He makes it clear: He doubts Eve's ability to resist Satan on her own. In response, Eve bites the inside of her cheek. She is hurt by Adam's lack of faith in her. She hates that he views her as incapable.

She silently wonders if love is always supposed to feel this stifling.

Eventually, Adam agrees to let Eve enjoy some solitude, and Eve wanders away by herself.

Meanwhile, Satan takes on the body of a serpent and nestles behind a bush. He waits for Eve to walk past. Her footsteps cause his scales to flicker with glee.

When Satan first approaches Eve, he struggles to capture her attention. She is lost in her own thoughts, pondering so many questions surrounding her new world.

Then Satan speaks to Eve in a haunting and intoxicating voice. He guides her to the forbidden tree. He tries to flatter her, calling her beautiful, stunning, precious, telling her that everyone deserves to see her beauty. But Eve remains guarded. She resists Satan's words, so he resorts to other tactics. He thinks hard for a moment, closing his eyes.

Satan then tells Eve that if she eats from the forbidden tree, she could be like God.

This sentiment sparks Eve's interest. Her eyebrows rise. Sweat glistens against her forehead, and a smile reaches her eyes for the very first time. She looks longingly at the forbidden tree. She imagines the deep well of possibility that lies inside its fruit. Perhaps the fruit could create a world where she doesn't have to ask Adam for permission . . . a world where there are no foods that she cannot eat . . . a world where she is not confused by her sexual desire . . . a world where her existence isn't defined by restraint. Maybe a single taste could build a real paradise.

Eve finally plucks the apple from its branch and takes a lavish bite.

⌒

I continued my way through the verses. I watched the garden tremble as a result of Eve's transgression. I did not want to finish the reading. I did not want to see Eve face any harm.

But I knew what was coming.

⌒

When I was a child, I used to pray for my panic attacks to go away. Although I was baptized Catholic, I grew up without having particularly close ties to any formal religion, so I invented my own God. I imagined that he looked like a handsome combination of my grandfathers—a tall man with wrinkled skin, thick glasses, and a charming Uruguayan accent. I spoke to this invented God every night before I fell asleep.

I would think: *Dear God, please make my heart feel better tomorrow.*

Usually, I pressed my face into the fabric of my pillowcase. I whispered my one-sentence prayer three times in a row. Praying always felt close to magic—like casting a small spell. I took comfort in the ritual. I believed that maybe, eventually, my prayers would build me an entirely different mind and an entirely different body. Maybe my heart could stop hurting. Maybe my thoughts would calm down.

At some point, the prayer adapted into a shorter phrase. I started whispering the new version before I fell asleep, a humble chant: *Dear God, dear God, dear God.*

I still believed the repetition could stop the panic, but I held less faith in the exact words.

Later on, I gave up on words altogether. I just counted myself to sleep: *One, two, three. One, two, three.*

And you already know how the rest of the story goes. Like Eve, I lived in a world where I tried to whittle myself down. Like Eve, I had to try to fit into a set of rules that I had no part in creating. Only certain foods. Only certain desires. Only one kind of love.

But eventually I realized that sometimes our gods—the gods we invent in our heads and the gods we read about in our stories and the gods who show up in our high school history classes—they don't always know what's best for us.

When I reached the last line of our assigned reading, I looked out my favorite library window. The sun was beginning to dim behind Colorado's mountains. A group of students was laughing in the courtyard. My heart was beating slowly, calmly.

I grabbed my pen and inserted myself back into the story.

Inside my copy of *Paradise Lost,* I let my handwriting sloppily curl across a page. I wrote down a new prayer:

> *Dear Eve,*
>
> *Thank you for teaching me that I cannot keep trying to build paradise out of all the things I've kept from myself.*

22

The Fitting

"Wave at the camera!" I ordered Joe. I chuckled and held my phone up to his face.

"It's too early for this," he groaned back.

It was five in the morning, but I was wide awake. We were sitting together inside the Colorado Springs Airport. The terminal was empty except for a few travelers carrying to-go cups of coffee and pulling suitcases across the tiled floor. We watched a couple of planes take off outside the window and eagerly waited to board our own flight. Joe and I were about to head to our first event as a part of Team USA.

We had received the news a couple of weeks earlier.

After a string of successful competitions, U.S. Figure Skating had decided to take a chance on us: We were being sent to the Autumn Classic International, a senior-level competition in Canada, where we would compete against other teams from all over the world. Being named to Team USA meant that we could attend certain international events and were eligible for certain funding opportunities. It also meant that I would finally get to wear a red-white-and-blue jacket. I would finally get to hear my name announced alongside the words *Representing the United States of America* . . .

It seemed like I had been working my entire life to board this plane and take part in this particular adventure. I wanted to document every second of the experience—which is why I was begging Joe to wave at my camera.

"I never want to forget how happy I am right now," I said. "No matter what happens at the competition."

"I know what you mean," Joe said. He finally gave me a wave. "Let's just try to have fun."

And we did have fun.

When we showed up at the arena, I probably looked more like a fan than a competitor. I walked around the stands wide-eyed, dressed head to toe in my Team USA gear. I took pictures everywhere I went. Joe bounced through the hallways, cheerfully greeting our teammates with hugs. We giggled together at our practices, and we joked around with our competitors in the locker rooms, and somehow—by some beautiful twist of fate—we walked away from the competition with a bronze medal.

As I stepped onto the podium next to Joe, tears welled in my eyes.

I felt unstoppable. I could picture my future assembling: more international competitions, more medals, more traveling and meeting new friends. Maybe in the future, we could go to an even bigger event—a Grand Prix . . . or the Olympics! Anything could happen!

But the day after we got home, someone took a match to my hopes.

Back in Colorado Springs, one of my coaches pulled me aside at practice. My coach's face had a grave expression, and I knew something was wrong. The air went rancid. I felt like I was stuck inside a horror movie, trapped in the moment right before the monster jumps out. I stared at my feet. In the calmest voice, my coach said that I looked *too heavy* at the competition, and those words caused my hard-earned pride to curdle inside my stomach.

After years of working to heal all the heartache tied up in my shape, my body had continued to change. My hips had widened. My chest had grown. I had gotten used to being the softest-looking girl in the locker room—but I finally understood that my appearance was not connected to my athletic ability in any way. I finally understood that my skills were virtually unaffected by the normal growth of my body. In fact, coercing my body into its smallest form pretty much always made my skating worse.

I wanted to yell at my coach. I wanted to scream: *I just won a medal! I'm not too heavy! I swear!* But instead, I nodded, fighting back tears.

When I got home from practice, I stepped on a scale for the first time in years. I pinched at the sides of my belly, and I considered the devastating possibility of skipping dinner. *I can fix this,* I thought. *I can make myself small again.*

But then I took a few deep breaths, and I remembered how far I had come. I remembered all the reasons why I gave up starving.

I called another coach—a ballet instructor who worked at our rink. She had always been kind to me. She smelled like lavender and spoke in a soft voice. She seemed like one of the few adults at the rink I could trust.

We brainstormed options together. I believed that confronting my coach was out of the question. I was too worried about backlash . . . too worried that I would be labeled as someone uncoachable and difficult. Going on a diet was out of the question too. I knew that dieting would summon my old demons from their depths.

"What if we have your costumes altered?" the ballet teacher suggested. "You won't have to lose any weight, but a few alterations might make you look smaller at your competitions. It might appease your coach a little bit?"

"I guess I can probably live with that," I said.

A couple days later, I was standing in a local seamstress's studio carrying two rhinestone dresses in my arms.

My mom had sewn my costumes that year. In an effort to save money, she had spent hundreds of hours on YouTube, learning the ins and outs of her sewing machine—and she had done a really good job. I loved both of my dresses. The first was a dark, melancholy gown with intricate layers of black tulle and glittering sections of lace that fell off my shoulders. The second was a playful, short-skirted number made from black, white, and red fabric. It reminded me of something a circus performer might wear for a tightrope walk. Polka dots spotted the fabric's bust. A giant red bow covered my butt. When I wore the costumes, I felt pretty. Sparkling. Protected from the world somehow. But as I carried them into the seamstress's studio, I felt a lurch of dread. I didn't want to put them on. I didn't want to be reminded of the reason I had scheduled the alterations in the first place.

The seamstress welcomed me at her front door and guided me through a series of rooms. Wedding gowns and prom dresses hung from every wall. Fabrics in a million shades and textures were draped over tables and chairs—I resisted the urge to reach out and caress a molten silk that had been strewn over a desk. Sequins like the scales of exotic Technicolor fish were sorted in various containers. The whole studio looked as if my childhood dress-up bin had run away and taken on a life of its own.

When I started skating as a kid, I loved choosing my own costumes. My very first skating dress was a pink crushed-velvet number with a she'll-grow-into-it fit. At six years old, I asked my mom to sew a feather boa onto the sleeves because I had seen Oksana Baiul skate in a feather-laden dress on TV. The end result was a ridiculous and adorable outfit—a unique creation that made me feel superhuman when I put it on (although I probably looked less like a superhero and more like a bubble-gum chicken). As I got older, I stayed heavily involved in the dressmaking process—sketching out designs on scraps of paper with my mom and carefully gluing patterns of gleeful rhinestones onto our creations. But at some point, the procedure lost its magic. My coaches started getting involved. Judges started making notes. I was told not to wear halter dresses because they made my boobs look too big. I was told not to wear white because the color emphasized the rolls of my stomach. I was told not to wear shorts or pants because they were against the rules. (Yes—in the sport of ice dance, there are rules against women wearing pants.)

By the time I walked into the seamstress's studio, I had learned to dread costume discussions.

The seamstress guided me to a fitting room and told

me to call her over when I was ready. I slipped into the short-skirted dress. I turned around in the mirror a few times and pulled at the bow covering my butt. I plucked at the straps looping over my shoulders. I tried to suck my stomach in and press my boobs closer toward my chest. *My coach is right,* I thought. *I don't look like a figure skater.* I bit down against the urge to cry.

"Are you ready?" the seamstress asked.

I wiped beneath my eyes with my thumbs.

"I'm good," I said. "You can come in."

I took a few deep breaths to usher the redness out of my face. The seamstress pushed aside the fitting-room curtain. She carried a few safety pins in her hands.

"The dress is adorable," she said. "What exactly are we looking to fix?"

And with that, I lost all sense of composure. *We're looking to fix me,* I thought, but—of course—I didn't say that out loud. I didn't say anything out loud. I just cried like the emotional, overflowing girl that I was.

Before I knew it, the seamstress was wrapping me up in her arms, and she was offering me a box of tissues, and it occurred to me that I wasn't the first girl who fell apart while standing in front of these mirrors—not at all. The fitting room was filled with satin-clad ghosts: ballerinas who asked for their tutus to be let out and bridesmaids who weren't flattered by the fit of their dresses. I thought about how mirrors had acquired a reputation for holding on to bad luck, and I thought about how that little piece of mythology suddenly seemed to make a whole lot of sense.

"Let me guess," the seamstress said. "Your coach thinks you don't look thin enough?"

I nodded.

"Well . . . I have a few tricks we can try." She sighed. She began poking pins into different parts of the fabric, and she drew chalky lines near my hip bones, and I stood mannequin-like while she worked. Within ten minutes, the safety pins had managed to hourglass my body. At least an inch of my waist disappeared into the light.

"What do you think?" the seamstress asked.

"I look a little slimmer," I said. "My coaches will be happy. The judges will be happy."

"I want *you* to be happy too," the seamstress said.

I didn't quite know how to respond. Disappearing had never brought me happiness—only something close to relief—but standing in the fitting room, I didn't exactly feel relief either. I felt more like I had made a cursed bargain. I had entered the studio and allowed a piece of my waist to be erased so my life could be a little easier . . . so my coach would leave me alone . . . so I could boost my shot at winning more medals. But what kind of deal was that?

It's tough to say.

For elite athletes, our environment constantly offers us a question: *What are you willing to give up to get ahead? What are you willing to sacrifice?*

When I was young and naive and hungry, I would have answered, *Everything*. But my answer had slowly started to shift. Sometimes, I dared to ask questions back: *What does it really mean to get ahead? Who am I leaving behind?*

I stood at the mirror and looked at myself. The neckline of my dress puckered into a sweetheart, visually breaking up the shape of my chest. The skirt slanted into a V shape where the fabric met my waist, slimming the appearance of my belly and my hips. I sucked in my stomach and held my breath. The dress was still the same gorgeous dress my mother had made—just a little different. The body in the mirror was still the same soft and curving body I had possessed an hour before—just a little hidden.

"I'm happy enough," I said to the seamstress.

I am leaving pieces of myself behind, I thought.

The parts of my body that had been erased by the alterations were abandoned inside the fitting room. The mirrors held on to my secrets. And now you hold on to them too.

Spoiler: If you think I am always the good guy in this book, I've allowed you to be misled until now. If I am anything at all, I am a human being built entirely of gray areas. In this story—in *most* stories—I am both the victim and the perpetrator; I am never sure of my own footing; I am full of second guesses.

You have to remember—while I was competing, I still

23

My Boyfriend Told Me
I Was a Lesbian

Daniel appeared in my life the same way clouds roll in during a summer storm—as if conjured by daydreams and galaxies. Joe and I were practicing at our usual ice rink, which was located inside the Air Force Academy, when a couple of cadets walked in.

Joe and I were heading into our second season on Team USA, and we skated with a newfound confidence. We glided across the rink with more speed. I practiced with my hair down, and the wind trailed it behind me.

The cadets paused to watch us skate and clapped as we carved our way around the ice. I liked having an audience, even a small one. Joe and I looked up at the cadets

217

occasionally, performing more than we would have had we been alone. Our little audience hung around, pointing and cheering for an entire hour. Eventually, Joe and I stepped off the ice to take a break. While we sat on the bleachers and unlaced our skates, the pair of cadets approached us.

"Y'all are really good," one of the boys said. He was tall, and his features were noticeably kind. He had a faintly Texas-sounding lilt to his voice. The other cadet stood a few paces behind, looking around the room shyly.

"Thanks," Joe and I both replied at the same time.

"It's nice to meet you," I added.

Joe and I had been through this a few times already. Every once in a while, cadets wandered in and tried to strike up conversations with us while we trained.

"So are you two competing in Rio?" The tall cadet's eyes wandered to our Team USA jackets.

I giggled. "Rio is hosting the Summer Olympics. Skating happens during the winter ones. . . ."

Looking slightly embarrassed, the cadet blushed a sheepish, air-warming blush. He laughed, apologized. His friend stifled a snort.

"Don't worry about it. We actually get asked that all the time. It happened just the other day when I wore my jacket to the grocery store."

We made small talk for a few more minutes before Joe and I had to hop back onto the ice. The cadets walked off to their classes, but I made sure to wave before they disappeared out the door.

"The tall one who asked about the Olympics was cute," I said to Joe wistfully. "I should have gotten his number."

"You never know—he might come back tomorrow," Joe replied.

Luckily, I didn't have to wait that long. That night, I got a message on Instagram:

Hey. This is Daniel. I'm the guy from the ice rink this morning. I thought you were really genuine and cute, and I was wondering if you wanted to go on a date sometime?

We met up a few nights later. We sat across from one another at a chain Italian restaurant, and we both fidgeted with our silverware. Daniel barely touched his pasta because he was worried about *eating weird or spilling something* (an insight he revealed to me weeks later). Our waitress couldn't help but give us doting looks throughout the night. Apparently, it was obvious that we were brand-new to our romance.

For the rest of the evening, all our actions dripped with intentional sweetness. After dinner, we walked across the street to a place where we could play mini golf and arcade games. Despite my lifelong competitive streak, I didn't keep track of scores. Instead, I watched Daniel putt a blue golf ball into a windmill, and I imagined spending an entire summer with him. We paid a few dollars to enter some batting cages, and I only managed to hit one solitary base-ball, but I still took this as a sign of good luck.

I was so charmed, everything looked like a sign of good luck.

At the end of the night, Daniel and I sat next to each other, trying to muddle through the awkward conventions of saying good night. He told me that he'd had a great time, and I leaned toward him with a tentative swell of bravery. It felt good to be the one initiating a kiss. I think Daniel was pleasantly surprised. I felt him smile under-neath my mouth.

Within a matter of weeks, we officially started dating.

I relished the fact that I could call him my boyfriend. Having Daniel made me feel as though the adolescent, wallflowery version of myself was finally being swooned over.

We found ourselves giddy whenever we occupied the same space. I was usually busy with training, and he was usually busy with summer classes, so we spent most of our time looking forward to weekends, when he borrowed his sister's car to drive over to my house.

One Friday night, he showed up at my doorstep with chocolate cake mix and a dozen red roses in hand. I felt like I should have been embarrassed by the gesture—I gen-erally thought of myself as someone too distant, too artsy to fall for rom-com-like tactics—but his earnestness won me over, and I couldn't keep myself from smiling.

Together, we ate the cake batter before it was fully cooked. Our spoons spilled over with gooey, dripping batter. The kitchen light ushered a dull shine onto our faces, and we laughed at the way our blossoming affection made everything in our lives feel young and easy. Like the only things in the whole world that mattered were our small romantic tokens: my hair ties on his wrist, his borrowed car keys on my counter, the roses in their vase.

We giggled shamelessly when my roommate left for her night shift at work, knowing we would have the house to ourselves for the rest of the night.

Almost as soon as the door clicked shut, we entangled ourselves on the couch—a mess of legs and skin. We made out the way teenagers do in movies. One moment, we were lost in our own heavy breathing. The next, we were shut-eyed and curled close. As we rolled and collapsed into one another, he paused to touch the dip of my cheek's dimple. He brushed my skin with more affection than I could comprehend. I hadn't realized my body could be felt so gently. His tenderness almost scared me, but I also never wanted him to move his hand away. . . .

The night hours became indistinguishable. We clung to each other to keep from falling off the couch. I tucked my body on top of his and interlaced our fingers. We lay there for a moment, our chests rising and falling together.

"Okay, so who's your celebrity crush?" Daniel asked me, breaking our syrupy silence.

"What do you mean?"

"You know what I mean. There's got to be some famous guy who you would leave me for if he asked."

I laughed and paused to think.

"I'm not really planning on leaving you anytime soon. What's this even about?"

"Well, you don't have any exes who I can stalk online. . . . I'm just trying to get a feel for your type."

It was true. While Daniel had past relationships he could tell me about, I had only a brief history of boys in dorm rooms and halfway-formed flirtations that never amounted to much. I hardly had enough of a track record to pin down a *type*. I took a deep breath and pondered for a few minutes.

"I kind of have a thing for Zayn Malik. You know . . . from One Direction," I said.

"I don't know who that is," he said.

My face twisted into an expression of feigned horror. "I can't believe I'm dating someone who doesn't even know the members of One Direction."

"Aren't they broken up?" he asked.

I gasped. "Don't speak of their breakup in front of me! There's always hope for a reunion!"

Daniel rolled his eyes, but his smile reached to the creases of his forehead. I could tell he was genuinely interested in all the versions of me that had existed before I met him, and his attention made my stomach flutter. I pulled up pictures of Zayn on my phone, scrolling through to find the ones that were the most flattering.

"Hmm . . . he's all right," he said.

"Okay, so who is your celebrity crush? You must have one too."

We had been lying pressed against each other, but I sat up and started to trace the curves of his chest with my finger. He smelled so clean and simple—like soap or fresh sheets. I shut my eyes. I figured he would have to think for a moment too, but he came up with an answer almost immediately.

"Easy. Selena Gomez."

"No way! Me too," I said excitedly.

"Selena Gomez is your celebrity crush?" His eyebrow lifted into a question.

"Sure. She's got a really cute face. I have lots of celebrity girl crushes," I said casually. I didn't even think about how easily the words fell out of my mouth. I never considered my girl crushes to be gay crushes, so confessing them didn't feel like a newsworthy assertion. Besides, didn't all girls—didn't *everyone*—have at least a small crush on Selena Gomez?

"You had to think for like five minutes to come up with one male celebrity crush, but you have"—he paused to change his voice so as to indicate air quotes—"lots of celebrity girl crushes?"

"Yeah. Rihanna, Carey Mulligan, Cara Delevingne—"

Daniel interrupted me before I could go on.

"Are you *sure* you're not a lesbian?"

We both laughed. I made a show of looking down at our bodies, nearly bare and still touching.

"I don't think I'm a lesbian," I said. If I had possessed the confidence to wink at him, I would have. Instead, I just leaned in closer for a kiss.

We spent our night pressed together, talking about other minor secrets we had. We chatted about our favorite places in the world and our least favorite foods, and we tried to come up with questions that would excavate our pasts so we could share them with one another.

After that night, I'm almost positive, Daniel forgot about the celebrity-crush conversation. We went about our relationship as if my potential lesbianism had never floated into our view.

I could have easily let the playful accusation slide from my memory too. It wasn't the first time I had ever talked about my extensive list of girl crushes. I had revealed the list to various female friends without a second thought, and none of them had seemed to bat an eyelash, but something changed when I heard the word *lesbian* said out loud in my direction. I found myself oddly flattered. I liked the way the word sounded, like part of a poem; I liked the way the word looked when I wrote it down (sometimes, in my journal, I found myself writing it down).

But I really liked Daniel, so it was easy to brush off any

feelings of doubt that crept into my subconscious. I told myself to worry about it another time, and I kept looking forward to Friday nights and grocery-store roses for a while. Our affection felt endless and warm.

When summer ended, Joe and I got to compete at the second international event of our careers, and we scored within a few points of teams that had actually gone to the Olympics. I began to think Daniel's initial question had truly been a good-luck charm. When I returned to Colorado Springs, I looked out at the mountains—and as clichéd as it sounds, I was sure I was living at the very top of the world.

24

The Breakup

When January arrived, I left town for a week to compete at the national championships in Kansas City.

Joe and I skated well, and we were relieved to reach the end of our season. It had been a challenging one—our program had been a bit too difficult for us, and even though we were growing stronger as skaters, we had made several mistakes that kept us from scoring as well as we wanted to at sectionals. At nationals, we felt like we had won the lottery just by making it through our programs without any major blunders.

During the week I was away, I noticed that Daniel's

texts became shorter and less frequent, but I figured he was giving me space to focus on the competition.

I didn't mind the space, but when I arrived back in Colorado, I was eager to exchange details about our week apart. I called Daniel as soon as I exited the airplane. My suitcase clicked behind me while I waited for him to pick up.

I had missed him while I was away.

When his voice hummed through my phone, I could tell something was wrong. His greeting sounded guarded and jumpy. Maybe he was just tired? Nervous? Regardless, my mind couldn't shake the tension. We talked for a few minutes about the competition and the start of the new semester, and I tried to fake a sense of ease, but I had never been very good at playing things casually. Eventually, our conversation wavered into an uncomfortable silence, and I couldn't stop myself from asking, "Is something wrong?"

"I was hoping we could talk about it in person," he said.

The next morning, I checked my phone. Daniel and I had gotten into the habit of sending text-message *I love yous*, but I was disappointed to find that there weren't any notifications waiting for me when I woke up.

A few days later, we met outside the Air Force Academy's ice rink. I had just finished practicing. Daniel had just gotten out of class. We wandered through the parking lot in silence. I waited to hear bad news.

Daniel started to explain that he had been accepted into a study-abroad program. He would be staying in South America for a year, and even if our relationship could survive the year apart, he would then graduate and subsequently fly off to another base somewhere else in the world. He didn't want to spend an entire relationship separated by distance. I didn't want to follow him around; I had my own plans, and I had my own reservations. I had competitions to prepare for, homework to finish, big, impossible dreams for myself (and I had a curiosity regarding the word *lesbian* that had been rumbling at the back of my belly for months). In the end, the breakup was mostly mutual, but he was the one who said it out loud.

I wanted to be angry with him, but I couldn't muster up the energy.

Instead, I went home and put on a sweatshirt he had given me and cried to weepy Taylor Swift songs. I spent the rest of the week eating ice cream in bed. For an entire month, I drove around listening to playlists of his favorite songs. I felt like girls I never used to understand—the ones who couldn't remember who they were when they were alone. For so long, I had prided myself on not needing anyone. Nobody had ever been in love with me and I had managed to keep existing! But once I experienced connecting with someone—the wholeness of it, the feeling of being adored—I tumbled into a kind of withdrawal.

This was my problem: I did everything wholeheartedly. When I was alone, I committed to being completely alone. When I was in love, I wanted that love to eat me alive.

"It can't be that bad. It's not like he cheated on you or anything," a friend told me while I was basking in my hurt. He had come over to my house to try to cheer me up. We baked cupcakes in my kitchen and sipped on cans of iced tea. I had clearly been wearing the same sweater for too many days. The waves of my hair were collected into a greasy bun.

"I wish he had cheated on me or done something wrong," I said. "I want to be able to feel angry at him, but I just feel sad."

"I know it seems like it's too soon, but you should get on a dating app. It'll make you feel better."

My friend was already building a profile for me before I could resist.

We sat at my kitchen table and swiped through nearly all the eligible bachelors of Colorado Springs. Despite a few matches, I felt wildly uninspired.

"Maybe I'm just not ready," I told my friend.

He looked disappointed by my lack of enthusiasm. "I'm not saying you have to find your soul mate. I'm just saying you have to stay open to new possibilities," he insisted.

That night—after my friend had gone home and my

roommate had gone to bed—I stayed awake and drew doodles in my journal. I couldn't sleep. My legs didn't want to hold still. I sat up and clicked through my phone. I went back to swiping through the dating app. I continued feeling disenchanted, but swiping seemed like a better way to kill the time than putting on Daniel's sweatshirt and making myself sad all over again.

As I swiped, an instinct took over.

I remember the rest of the night as the only out-of-body experience I've ever known. It was as if my fingertips were moving without any agency or impulse control. After paging through hundreds of photos of men, I watched myself stop, and I saw my hand pull up the setting controls on the app. Without thinking at all, I changed my status from *seeking men* to *seeking women*.

As pictures of women appeared, I noticed my pulse restarting.

I only stared at the pictures. I didn't try to match with anyone—I didn't want to do anything too real or too concrete. Instead, I admired the women from afar. Even with the careful distance that I kept, I couldn't deny the magnetic force of my body. Looking at pictures of long hair and nose piercings and gloss-covered lips . . . I realized how possible it could be to fall in love with someone new.

Then I fell asleep.

In the morning, I woke up to a world-ending sort of

dread. I switched my app's settings back to men. When that wasn't enough to calm my terror, I deleted the app entirely.

For weeks, I started getting panic attacks so intense and frequent, I thought they might really be heart attacks.

25

The Leap

When most people picture Arizona, they picture sepia tones. They picture cacti, and red rocks, and sultry summer heat. They imagine tumbleweeds rolling along a dusty road. These images aren't necessarily wrong, but Arizona has another side.... The state contains oases if you choose to follow a cool breeze and drive toward the horizon.

During the early spring, my friends and I spent weeks planning a trip to visit some of Arizona's waterfalls.

The skating off-season was in full swing, and I managed to get some time away from training. Everyone would be there—all the girls I had grown up with, and some new friends who had become permanent staples in our little cohort. Even though we'd gone to different colleges after graduation, our rapturous ties from high school remained. Still the coordinator of our bunch, Rayna had meticulously organized the details of our reunion.

I flew to Arizona, and my friends arrived at my house within an hour.

We piled into Nati's car and drove along miles of ribboning highway. We bickered over who controlled the aux cord. We shared bags of chips and bottles of Gatorade. Our voices escalated, shouting with adrenaline and joy as if we were sixteen again. Tidbits of our lives slipped out. We raced to catch up on everything that had happened since we'd splintered off in different directions: Everyone wanted to travel overseas; everyone had flirtatious stories to tell; everyone planned to change the world someday.

The views along the drive were full of wasteland and sky. For long stretches, there were hardly any houses or other buildings to block our gaze. When I looked out my window, I could have sworn I saw the very edge of the earth. Rayna's sleeping head rested on my shoulder, and I tipped my own head so it puzzle-pieced perfectly on top of hers.

We arrived at a parking lot near the base of a mountain. After a quick stop at a visitors' center to collect a few maps, we began the four-mile hike toward the falls.

Our feet stomped in rhythmic unison. We sang songs along the way, rekindling lyrics from our past. Fellow hikers smiled as we walked by. The unmistakable sun-screen scent drifted along each gust of wind. Every once in a while, we stopped to document the adventure, pulling our phones from our backpacks to snap a few shots.

I knew we were nearing the falls when I heard the distinctive splashing of water. It started off gentle—like a faucet left on in another room—but the noise grew until it became a rush of thunder and mist.

We stood at the bottom of the waterfalls. Each basin poured into the next.

The scene reminded me of our friendship: all the years we had spent overflowing and catching each other.

We stripped down to our sports bras and shorts. Nati rushed off, barefooted. She was determined to climb one of the highest cliffs and then dive into the water. Mackenzie and Lindsay ran after her. There were two boys who had made their way into our clan, Patrick and Jason, and they tagged along behind the girls.

"I'll just wait at the bottom with Rayna and take your pictures," I insisted.

"You're going to regret it if you don't jump!" Nati called back at me.

"She's right," Rayna chimed in. "You're going to feel bad if you don't join them."

I couldn't argue with her, so I tentatively followed my friends.

Getting to the edge of the cliff was a challenge in its

own right. There were no clear paths to follow. We had to climb over boulders and jump between gaps where the stream had washed away sections of earth. I made someone hold my hand every time I was forced to balance on a rickety stepping-stone. As we trekked upward, the basins began to look farther and farther away. Giant pools of water became clay-colored puddles as our vantage point changed.

Nati arrived at the ledge first. There was no fear in her eyes. She took a running start and cannonballed without a second thought. Her body hurled itself toward the water. The thrash of the falls churned behind her. She plummeted below the surface.

We all watched with terror and fascination.

Then Nati's head bobbed back up, and she flung her hair behind her, and she laughed with a spectacular cackle.

"Come on!" she yelled. "Jump in!"

Oh god, I thought. *There's no way I'm jumping in.*

I couldn't get down from the ledge the way I got up—the route was too treacherous. My eyes darted, searching for a way to exit the cliff that didn't involve diving into the water, but there was no way out. I was trapped.

A breeze passed by, and I had a vision of the wind blowing me into the water before I was ready. I imagined my body slipping and crashing into rocks along the way down. I clutched at Patrick's arm and lowered myself to the ground. My mind spun. My heart stuttered. A familiar series of what-if questions appeared: *What if I forget how to swim when I hit the water? What if I can't even bring myself to jump? What if I find myself stuck on this cliff for the rest of my life? What if I have a heart attack right here?*

Mackenzie was about to dive into the water, but when she noticed my sudden alarm, she turned around and walked back to me.

"It'll be fine," she said. "I'll go first and show you that it's okay."

Lindsay wrapped her arms around my shoulders.

I closed my eyes. I reminded myself of some breathing techniques and methods to slow my heart rate. I inhaled steadily. I imagined an ice cube was melting on my palm. I tried to feel its cool edges, and I waited until the made-up object had dissolved in my hand.

When I opened my eyes, my friends were still there.

"Think of the story you'll have when this is over," Lindsay remarked.

She knew I was a sucker for a good story. I stood up, and I walked closer to the ledge. When I looked down, I saw that Nati was still wading around the cusp of the pool. Rayna sat on a patch of adjacent dry land, kicking her toes through the water.

Mackenzie and Lindsay counted to three.

Then they took off together, soaring and flailing. They landed with a remarkable splash and swam to meet Nati and Rayna. I watched my friends giggle and sparkle and towel the water from their hair, and I thought I might be witnessing a group of mythical desert-dwelling mermaids.

My mind started churning again. *Why am I always so scared? What if all my friends hate me for being this anxious? What if they secretly wish I had not come along? What if they all realize that I'm gay?*

The last thought kicked my lungs.

Before I could fall back into panic, I turned to Patrick.

"Jump in with me?" I asked.

"Let's do this," he said.

I looked across at the horizon line and told myself to aim there. I leaped out as far as I could. The water came, and it was nothing like a death. Ripples cascaded around me. A glistening piece of sun crackled along the surface above me.

And then I broke through, laughing. I could hear my friends cheering before I even emerged from the water.

26

The Closet and Misunderstanding Quantum Mechanics

When I returned to Colorado, I knew it was time to inch my way out of the closet.

I felt energized after seeing my friends. They kept pushing me to do things that scared me. They never let me give in to my panicky thoughts. If the trip home had proved anything, it was that the five of us would always have an inseparable connection. . . .

But I also had some reservations.

I worried that the dynamics of our relationships would change after I admitted my feelings for women. I feared my friends' potential hesitations, often questioning myself in the middle of the night: *Would Rayna become uncomfortable with the clothes that I borrowed from her closet? Would Lindsay regret the sleepovers that we spent in the same bed? Would Mackenzie and Nati feel weird about the intimate notes and letters that we wrote one another? Would all my dearest friends suddenly question our closeness?*

Before I could talk myself out of coming out, I sent a quick text to our group chat.

I miss you guys already, I wrote.

Lindsay responded first. *I miss you already too, friend.*

I messaged her privately.

Can I call you tonight?

Of course, she replied.

When I called, my voice came out shaky and dramatic. Lindsay's face bobbed inside my phone screen. My whole body fell victim to an aggressive sweat.

"I have something to tell you," I said.

"Are you okay?" Lindsay asked. She could already sense my panic.

"Yeah, yeah, I'm fine. . . . I'm just going to say it." I took a deep breath. "Okay, so I think I might be . . . into girls." My eyes danced around my room, unsure of where to focus. Lindsay smiled back at me through the blue light of our video chat.

"That's amazing," she said with a settling matter-of-factness.

"I was a little nervous. Because we're so close, and I don't want our friendship to start feeling weird—"

"Oh, stop," she interrupted. "I'd honestly be offended right now if you told me that you were attracted to women but weren't at least a little attracted to me. . . ."

I laughed because she was right. And it was that easy.

Within the next couple of weeks, I came out to the others: Rayna and Nati and Mackenzie. And each time, I felt a small bite of freedom—like I was waking from the heaviest sleep.

Everyone had a slightly different reaction. Rayna gave me a recommendation for a podcast that talked about LGBTQ+ politics; she was always learning, and she seemed to have an endless stream of resources for any situation. Mackenzie, who was the most religious of our group, talked to me about her faith, and we pieced together the ways that our identities could still support one another. Nati didn't seem too shaken by my confession at all, and our conversation quickly turned to other topics.

They each loved me so well. The only problem was that as I confessed my feelings, I never felt sure of what to come out as.

On our calls, I let my sentences tiptoe. I used generic expressions rather than specific labels. I said things like *I'm into girls, I have crushes on girls, I want to kiss girls.* Yet even those sentences failed to capture my particular condition. Perhaps a better explanation would have avoided gender entirely—perhaps a better explanation would have managed to grasp the sudden realization that my own capacity for attraction spanned across a much wider landscape than I had previously believed.

For so many years, I had worn *straight* without second-guessing its fit, but as I gained a clearer vision of myself, I struggled to decide which new word to put on. The absence of an identifier made me feel vulnerable and naked.

In order to sort out my feelings, I stayed up late one night, clicking at my laptop's keyboard, searching for something new to call myself. I drew the curtains shut and lit a candle. My ceiling fan whirred. I put on a playlist of Frank Ocean songs. My neighbors barbecued into the warmth of the night. I typed *list of sexualities* into Google's search bar and scrolled through dozens of websites. I happened upon so many words, each a little different from the one that came before.

My Google search offered so many labels to try on: *lesbian, bisexual, pansexual, fluid, questioning, queer.* I felt as if I had accidentally waded into the deep end of a pool.

I wrote the words down in my journal, tracing the letters in curvy pen strokes. I practiced saying the words out loud (softly enough to keep my roommate from hearing). There was something about every word that attracted me: I liked the way *lesbian* forced my tongue to brush against my teeth. I liked the way *fluid* seemed so akin to dancing—so similar to the feeling of skating. *Questioning* seemed to dictate my every thought: Who was I? Had I always been this way? Would I be this way forever?

I especially liked the word *bisexual.* Its definition seemed the closest to my reality: an attraction to people of my own and other gender identities.

Bisexual should have been the most practical option, but I was scared of the word. I didn't personally know anyone who was bisexual. I had never seen the word wielded outside of fiction, and I knew it carried a host of stereotypes: party girls, and indulgent villains, and fun-loving best friends. And a part of me wanted to be all those things! I wanted to be impulsive and free. I wanted to be the interesting character—the one full of mystery and power—but I didn't think I lived up to the role. And I was afraid to claim a middle space. I wanted assurance that my attraction to women would be unshakable. I wanted something concrete. I wanted a word that felt tangible, and permanent, and solidified. Bisexuality seemed to admit to a certain degree of flexibility.

I asked myself again: *Have I always been this way? Will I be this way forever?*

I hated the fact that my answer to both questions was: *I don't know.*

I went to bed unassured and indecisive. How could I encounter so many words and still not know which one to choose?

⌒

A few weeks later, I came across an article about quantum mechanics—I had been surfing the internet, reading one article that led to another that led to another. I was probably procrastinating on a homework assignment, and I googled a question that popped into my head: *Is it scientifically possible to exist in two places at once?* Maybe the question was just a random thought, or maybe the question arose from the depths of the unknown. Either way, I fell down a late-night Wikipedia rabbit hole. Before I knew it, I was reading paragraphs that could have been mistaken for science fiction.

The article talked about the ways that classical physics fails to sufficiently explain the behavior of the universe's smallest particles. In the 1920s, scientists discovered that electrons can actually exist in two places at once.

The tiniest bits of matter can live in a limbo space—an in-between. Sometimes electrons act like particles, and sometimes they act like waves.

Here's the craziest part: Nobody really understands why.

While I read, I kept thinking about how my body was made up of organs, which were made up of cells, which were made up of atoms, which all contained electrons. I thought about how—if I could be broken down into impossibly minuscule bits—I could exist in two places at once too.

Maybe I had the physics all wrong (I probably had the physics all wrong!), but the thought was still alluring. I imagined my own electrons dancing between planes of existence.

If I could be in two places at once, I could be *bisexual* and *queer* and *fluid* and *everything* all at the same time. Maybe I was a particle and a wave—meant to live in the in-between and the not-easily-understood.

The idea gave me a reprieve from the constant indecision.

I stopped feeling so much pressure to narrow myself down to the pinprick of a single label. I needed to be thinking smaller than pinpricks—I needed to be thinking as small as electrons.

I could bend and change like a shadow. I could inhabit several words at once. I could thrive in my instability.

Sometimes the best answer we have is: *I don't know.*

Maybe I could simply understand myself in the

movement it takes to type out a sentence—rather than the words that eventually land on the page.

Spoiler! Here is something people don't always realize: Coming out is not an ending but an ongoing.

Even years after first testing the waters of *not straight,* I still need labels to explain myself to strangers. This isn't exactly a problem. We are all reaching for words to understand one another better (and to understand ourselves better!). We're all continuously changing and coming up short with our language, but we're trying anyway. That's just what humans do.

If you are struggling to claim a label for yourself, don't feel any pressure to rush. The words will always be there. They don't mind waiting.

After spending a few years as an out member of the LGBTQ+ community, I realized that I was not the only person who'd learned to understand myself better through the mysterious science of quantum mechanics. One of my friends who is nonbinary told me that quantum mechanics helped them make peace with their own queer identity. Quantum mechanics gave them a whole new view of reality—it allowed them to step into a world with a different set of rules and a more creative approach to gender. While we chatted about the messy paths that we had taken to make sense of ourselves, my friend showed me a video of Amrou Al-Kadhi, a writer and drag performer who has also used quantum mechanics to embrace the contradictory nature of queerness and celebrate the many delicious intersections of identity that exist in our world. While we watched the video, I felt comforted by the notion that we had all somehow stumbled on the same analogy to illustrate the hardest-to-explain facets of ourselves.

When I was first coming out, my lack of understanding seemed to taunt me. Because I was not sure how to describe myself, I worried that I was not actually queer. But now I know that uncertainty and instability are beautiful and necessary things. So many queer people learn to love themselves not in spite of uncertainty but *because* of it. Maybe the deepest blessing of queerness lies inside its complications. I think it's healthy to hold on to the idea that there is so much about ourselves—and so much about the world—that we have yet to comprehend.

These days, when I reach for a word, I use *bisexual* or *queer* because they are some of my favorite words. They are so close to my heart. The more I use them, the more permanent they begin to feel. Plus, they remind me of the most interesting characters on every TV show. They carry a history of people who came before—people who gave me a vision of the life I live now.

I think it's important to call myself *bisexual* because—at the end of the day—that is what I am.

But when individual words do not feel like enough, I

can point to the world outside myself. I can say something like this: *I don't always know how to explain my love, and sometimes I think other people have explained it better than I ever could. Have you ever thought about the fact that electrons can exist in two places at once? Have you ever heard a Frank Ocean song?*

27

A Living, Breathing Legend

A group of skaters gathered in the ice-rink bleachers between practice sessions. Summer competitions were nearing, but my heart was struggling to stay invested. The more comfortable I grew with my sexuality, the less I felt like I belonged in the skating world. Most of the time I felt like a fraud. I went through the motions of training, but I grappled to find the same competitive eagerness that I had always taken for granted.

I munched on a protein bar while I unlaced my skates.

The other skaters in the bleachers had been talking about a girl they all knew—somebody I was only peripherally aware of—who trained at a rink in a different state. I had been quietly listening to the conversation, tempted by their gossip.

"She used to be dating a guy, but I heard she's a lesbian now," one of the skaters mentioned.

My ears perked up even more.

"Okay, but that doesn't mean she's *a lesbian*," another skater said. "She could be bi."

"Oh, come on," the first skater said. "Bisexuality isn't real. You're either gay or you're straight. People who say they're bi are just in denial."

I picked at the wrapper of my protein bar. I remained on the fringes of the conversation—just close enough to hear, but not quite close enough to contribute.

Of course, I had faced my own struggles with the word *bisexual.* I had dealt with my own fear surrounding the middle-space kind of desire, but I had finally developed an appreciation for my own ambiguity. I had finally been able to admit that my feelings were not made up.

I'm real, I thought.

I felt an urge to say the words aloud, but I was exhausted from training. I was exhausted at the thought of having to offer myself up as proof.

I threw away the wrapper of my protein bar, and I laced up my skates once again.

When I got back on the ice, I could have sworn that

the wind passed straight through me. My skin took on a translucent quality whenever my body wasn't situated perfectly beneath the fluorescent lights.

A piece of me vanished for the rest of the day.

That evening, I had daydreams of the tooth fairy. I imagined gossamer wings disappearing midflight. I pictured the Loch Ness monster shrinking down to the size of an eel. I watched a ghost dissolve into mist. I caught a glimpse of a life with no space for wonder—no space for remarkable things beyond easy comprehension.

If we were all skeptics, then nobody would have any good stories to tell.

At our first summer competition—an international event in Lake Placid with several elite teams—Joe and I skated really well. For our rhythm dance, we performed a rumba full of hair flips and body rolls. For our free dance, we skated to love songs from the movie *Moulin Rouge!*

In the free dance, Joe and I pretended to fall in love. We were good actors. We gazed into one another's eyes. We dreamily embraced.

When the competition ended, I sat in the locker room surrounded by the other teams who had managed to squeak into the final warm-up group. My makeup was rose-hued. My hair was gathered into a French twist. I wore a regal gold dress.

We ended up in fifth place, with some of the highest scores we'd ever received.

I should have been happy. It was supposed to be a moment of celebration, a moment of success, but I felt the same strange experience of translucence—like nobody could truly see me. Like I had no idea what to believe in anymore.

28

Cherry ChapStick

In 2008, Katy Perry released "I Kissed a Girl." Her first hit single, the song catapulted Katy to fame.

I was in seventh grade when the track came out. The moms of my middle school carpool urgently tried to change stations whenever it came on the radio. They deemed the lyrics too inappropriate for our tender ears. Naturally, this only made us like the song more. We hummed the melody in class. We tapped our feet to the chorus. We found a way to keep singing when our parents couldn't hear us.

I originally met Malia in an English class, but I remet her on a queer dating app.

I sent a matchmaking heart to one of her photos, and we spiraled into a habit of texting and messaging and Snapchatting for weeks on end. Malia was spending the summer with her parents, who lived in a city fifty miles south of Colorado Springs, so all our early flirtations took place online.

I don't mind the long drive. I just want to see you, I messaged her.

I wish we didn't live so far away from each other, she messaged back.

It's okay, I told her. *It will just make things that much more exciting when we manage to go on a real date.*

An ellipses bubble appeared on my screen while I waited for her to respond.

I held my phone with both of my hands. I was sitting crisscross on my bed, my back leaning against the wall. *A real date,* I thought. Even though Malia and I had been flirting for several weeks, meeting up in person felt like crossing a line—like taking a significant step away from being straight. *A real date,* I thought again, and my heart raced with equal parts boldness and hesitation.

How does this Saturday sound? she finally wrote back. *I'll plan the whole thing!*

I wondered if Malia agonized over her messages the

same way I did—typing and retyping dozens of times, debating whether or not to use emojis or wondering if she would seem crazed for adding extra exclamation points.

I can't wait!! I replied to Malia. I added two exclamation points and pressed send before I could reconsider.

The next few days passed slowly. I counted down until the morning of our date.

In the opening scene of the "I Kissed a Girl" music video, several fishnet-and-lace-clad models are sprawled across the floor of a bedroom. Katy Perry lies on a silky bed. She wears a busty gold dress and high heels. She holds a kitten in her arms: *a pussycat.* We are probably supposed to smile at this joke. Later in the video, she wears black lingerie. She lip-syncs in a fake garden—maybe a strange, sexualized re-creation of Eden—still surrounded by tempting femmes. Her hair is curled. Her makeup is done (the song rages on about cherry ChapStick, but all the models seem to have heavily glossed lips). If a viewer were to turn their speakers off, the video could easily be mistaken for a Victoria's Secret commercial. Every once in a while, Katy drags her palm across her body—from the shaved contour of her calf to the accentuated curve of her breasts.

The entire time, Katy seems to be making eyes at someone behind the camera.

I recognize these eyes. I have made them myself. They seem to be the eyes of a woman trying to capture the attention of a man.

The night before my date with Malia, I spent a lot of time standing in my closet, trying to decide what I was going to wear. I typed *lesbian fashion* into Google's search bar, and I ended up scrolling through photos of tattooed women wearing plain T-shirts tucked into ripped jeans. Several pictures of Kristen Stewart glowed on my phone screen.

The clothes in my closet suddenly seemed too precious and juvenile. My hangers were covered with ill-fitting summer dresses and cardigans from high school. I grabbed a floral romper dangling from its hanger. I stepped into its bright fabric and moved toward my mirror to examine myself. My shoulders shrugged. I pulled at the edges of my shorts. I had worn the exact same outfit on a date with my ex-boyfriend, Daniel, and I had felt cute—sexy, even. He had unfastened the pearly buttons while we made out in the car. In my memory, the moment had felt scandalous and mature. But posing in the mirror in the same romper for a different date, I didn't feel sexy. I felt young and awkward. Mostly, I felt ashamed. I no longer looked like someone I recognized. I could barely remember a time when I felt sure of who I was.

What are you wearing? I texted Malia. . . . *To our date, I mean! I'm not trying to be gross,* I added.

Lol. . . . I haven't decided yet, babe, she wrote. *I'll send you a pic when I get ready tomorrow.* She added a winking face to the end of her message.

My stomach squeezed over the way Malia's voice sounded in her texts—just the slightest bit cocky. She often called me pet names: *babe, sweetheart, beautiful.* Late at night, she sometimes messaged to say she was thinking of me. Her confidence should have been assuring, but mostly, it made me feel like I had missed a reading assignment. She seemed so good at being gay. I was sure I would be playing catch-up for the rest of my life.

The next morning, Malia messaged me a picture of herself wearing a romper similar to the one I had considered wearing. I let out a breath I hadn't realized I'd been holding in.

You look great, I messaged back. *Can't wait to see you in a bit!*

I put on a pair of overalls and a white tee. I took several selfies before settling on one that I felt confident in sending to Malia.

On my way, I told her.

Oh my god! You're stunning! she replied. *Text me when you get to the park!*

I think it's important to note that in the "I Kissed a Girl" music video, Katy never actually kisses a girl. Not even once.

The long drive to the park calmed me a bit. I put on a playlist of lesbian musicians—mostly Tegan and Sara, because they were the only ones I knew of at the time. Something about singing along to love songs full of female pronouns helped me breathe. I turned up the volume to combat the noise of the wind ripping through my rolled-down windows. The sun was out. I could feel my cheeks warm pink. I hovered in the slow lane, and I danced in my seat, earning stares from the semi drivers who zoomed past my window.

When I arrived at the park, Malia was already standing outside her car. She grinned with anxious joy as I pulled into a spot. In person, she seemed less intimidating than the idea of her that I'd built up in my head. In real life, she wasn't a suave, all-knowing lesbian. (I found out on our date that she was not a lesbian at all, but instead a wary bisexual like me.) She sort of shifted her weight with caution as I approached her.

Her arms were full. An old-school picnic basket was hooked over one of her elbows, and a blanket was folded over the other. Her long black hair caught the sunlight, and when she flipped it over her shoulder, it radiated with the iridescent shimmer of an oil slick.

I offered to help carry her things, but she declined, so instead of helping, I walked next to her empty-handed. In my head, I worried about the space between us. All my internal questions concerned themselves with proximity: *Am I standing too close to her? Am I standing too far? Does the two feet between us make it seem like I'm only looking for friendship? Would I seem too eager if I moved a little closer?*

We eventually spread out our picnic blanket beneath a tree. A small river ran across the park, and young moms pushed strollers along its edge. An elderly couple fed birds beneath an umbrella. The air smelled like summer and sunblock—it reminded me of home. I closed my eyes, and I imagined that Malia and I were inside that famous French painting—the one where the whole scene is made up of little dots. I was sure I could feel each individual cell that simmered inside my skin.

Malia pulled veggie burgers out from her picnic basket. They were wrapped in tinfoil like little gifts. While we ate, we wiped ketchup from the corners of our mouths and held cans of lemonade that sweated in the heat. I set my hand down on the picnic blanket a few inches from Malia's leg. I wasn't sure if she noticed. I already knew that the line between friendship and romance could span the width of a thread. I wasn't quite sure what side of the line my hand fell against.

Our conversation picked up with the churning of the river. Our connection was natural—even easier than it had been online, and just like it had been when we'd chatted in class, months before. Malia told me about her summer. She had spent the long days with her younger sister, and she had been working a part-time job. She told me about how she hoped to get into med school after she finished undergrad. She wanted to be a surgeon—maybe an orthopedic surgeon, but she wasn't sure. I talked about my early-morning skating practices, and I talked about my late nights working at a day care, and I told her that some days I wanted to be the president, and some days I wanted to be a poet, and some days I had no idea what I wanted to be at all.

"I think it's cool," Malia said. "The fact that you're a competitive skater, but you have this whole other life too."

"Thanks," I said. "Well . . . sometimes it's cool. Sometimes I feel like I don't have a choice. I just have to keep all the different parts of myself separate, you know?"

Malia nodded like she completely understood.

Between our sentences and confessions, a straight couple who had been standing on the opposite side of the river locked lips with one another.

I clung to an aching awareness of my surroundings. I had been keeping track of every person whose eyes might have wandered toward our picnic blanket. There was the family tossing a football next to a neighboring tree. There was the old couple beneath the umbrella. The parade of young moms. The blissful citizens of suburbia had never appeared quite so menacing to me (a privilege I had been afforded because of the color of my skin and my gender identity and the general nature of my outward appearance). In that moment, I was forced to reckon with the dangers of being out. Malia and I probably looked like a pair of friends, but I couldn't keep myself from wandering into hypotheticals. *What if someone realizes that we are a little more than friends? What if we let our hands touch? What if someone gets angry? What if we cause a scene?*

I couldn't shake the feeling that Malia and I had something to hide. Even though the weather was perfect for a picnic, I wished that the sun would dim slightly—I wished that the tree would offer a tiny bit more shade to conceal the way my hand was sitting right next to Malia's knee.

The third verse of "I Kissed a Girl" contains a pair of infamous lines. Katy Perry sings of her experimentation: *It's not what good girls do / Not how they should behave.*

In an interview with *Glamour* ten years after the release of "I Kissed a Girl," Katy stated: "We've come a long way. Bisexuality wasn't as talked about back then, or any type of fluidity. If I had to write that song again, I probably would make an edit on it. Lyrically, it has a couple of stereotypes in it." Katy didn't mention specifically which lyrics she would change, but I am assuming these two lines are among the possible culprits.

The thing is, in suburban Chandler, Arizona, in 2008, the lines rang true. Kissing girls wasn't something good girls did. The carpool moms changed the radio station before we could even sing along.

And ten years later, on a picnic blanket in Colorado Springs, the world had changed a little bit, but the lines still felt true. The nearness of my hand to Malia's leg felt dangerous. I still felt like I was singing along to another song I wasn't supposed to be singing along to.

Malia opened a bag of potato chips, and we handed it back and forth, tasting the salt from our thumbs between passes. When our snacking and chatting died down, we listened to the lazy sounds of the river. Our lack of conversation wasn't awkward. We dwelled inside a comfortable kind of quiet.

"You probably have to drive back soon so you can make it to work, right?" Malia said. I wanted to stay with her longer, but she was right—I had to go.

"Yeah, I should head back now. I'll help you pack everything up," I said.

On the walk back to our cars, I carried the picnic basket and Malia carried the blanket. We each had a free hand. As we walked, we let our fingers brush and interlace. It felt nice to hold a hand the same size as mine. It felt natural.

When we got to my car, I turned to face Malia, and we kissed. It was quick—barely a peck—but we both pulled away a little shaky. I was stunned by how familiar the kiss felt. I had been expecting a different kind of softness and a different kind of butterflies, but I was taken aback by the fact that, with my eyes closed and my heart racing, I couldn't really tell much of a difference between boy lips and girl lips. Lips are just lips are just lips. . . .

"I had fun today," I said.

"Me too," she breathed back. We hugged quickly and hurried into our cars.

I could just barely taste the memory of her ChapStick. I liked it—the way it clung to me.

At the end of Katy's music video, she wakes up in bed next to her boyfriend. The whole scene—the models, the lingerie, the implied kisses that were never shown on camera—all of it is revealed to be a dream.

In seventh grade, I saw the music video for the first time while I was spending the night at a friend's house. My friend's parents had already fallen asleep, and we were watching some countdown show on MTV. When Katy's video wrapped up, my friend and I refused to make eye

contact with one another. We kept our faces glued to the
TV's screen.

"I want to try kissing a girl someday," my friend said.
"You know . . . sometime before I die."

"Yeah, me too," I said.

We turned the lights off and went to bed. The next
day, we got to wake up as if our conversation had never
happened.

The day after my date with Malia, I woke up to a *Good
morning* text, and I found myself on the other side of a
threshold. When I woke up, the entire world was different
for me.

I *had* kissed Malia, and I *had* liked it.

And yet my fingers hesitated when I picked up my
phone to reply to her text. I felt an irrepressible urge to de-
lete her number and forget about the whole thing. I didn't
have a road map for the life that came after kissing a girl,
so I tried to pretend the kiss had never happened.

Like the carpool moms reaching for their radio dials, I
tried to pretend the damage had not already been done. I
stopped answering Malia's texts. I didn't know what else to
do. I was scared.

It was no use, but for a while, I tried to tell myself it
had all just been a dream.

These days when I watch the "I Kissed a Girl" video, I find myself concerned with the well-being of the minor characters: the women passed out on the bedroom floor, the femmes posing sumptuously in Eden. I wonder what their lives look like when the party is over. I wonder if they text Katy Perry the next day with hopeful expectations.

I wonder how they manage to cope when Katy, inevitably, chooses not to respond.

I regret the way I treated Malia. I will probably carry these regrets forever.

Because the truth is, for a long time, while I was figuring myself out, I let shame slide off my back and onto other women's shoulders. I still couldn't get comfortable with the things that I wanted. For a while, I left other women alone to clean up the messes I made.

29

I Can't Hate My Body
If I Love Hers

Although I struggled with my own sense of commitment, I couldn't give up kissing girls. It took a while for me to believe that women's lips could last longer than one night. Several months passed before I really warmed up to the idea of having a *girlfriend,* but once I did, there was no turning back.

Aleena and I were snuggled on her velvet comforter, browsing through her Snapchat memories, when a picture from two years before appeared in the feed. It was a shameless mirror selfie: her shoulders flexed, ripped abs poking out from below a sports bra.

It was a lighthearted image, probably taken in a moment of bold self-confidence or made in an attempt to flirt with another girl. But she didn't laugh or reminisce when she saw it. Instead, her face fell.

"I wish I still looked like that," she said.

I turned to her. She was clad in a similar sports bra and propped up on her elbow so that her shoulder flexed in the same way as it did in the picture. She had identical flirty dimples dotting her cheeks. I laughed.

"Babe, you still look like that," I said.

She rolled her eyes, and I leaned in to kiss her forehead.

"You know what I mean," she said, glancing at her stomach, her thighs.

She was right. Her face was a little fuller. Her belly curved into her hips in a softer way than her jagged younger body once had. But the differences were barely noticeable. If anything, the softness only made her more stunning. I felt lucky to have my hands pressed to her hips.

Despite several delicate attempts to tell her that she was more beautiful now than in the picture, I conceded that my reassurance probably wouldn't make any difference. I knew because I had played the same comparison game with my old pictures.

I hardly had any photographs saved into my Snapchat

memories. Despite spending my teenage years incessantly communicating through the app, I almost never kept the photos, and when I did, I didn't often look back at them. In the years since, my body had changed more than Aleena's had, and I didn't like to reminisce about it.

The eating-disordered version of me had been almost entirely erased. I could no longer remember the calorie counts that once haunted me. I had not weighed myself in years. Old pictures held the only tangible glimpses of the fragile girl I used to be. They showed my cheeks slightly hollowed. My collarbones jutting. My hair hanging long and stringy, as if weighed down by my adolescent sadness. The spark was missing from all my camera-ready smiles.

I had worked so hard to gain back my weight and my strength. The person I was in those photographs was nothing like the person I had become. I had long since stopped skipping meals, but I still felt a pang of hurt when I came across images of my smaller self. While I didn't miss the years of self-loathing, it was hard to believe how bad the starving was when I happened upon mirror selfies in my camera feed.

Snapshots from my skinnier past didn't show the way I would faint after working out; they didn't show my bruised skin or the way my hair fell out in clumps. When I looked back at the old selfies, all I saw was the way the light caught my cheekbones back when my face was a little bit thinner.

I had met Aleena a few months earlier. I hadn't been looking to fall in love—I was still trying to figure myself out—but she almost immediately cleared up my questioning. I couldn't even begin to deny my attraction to her. She had a laugh that curled in and in on itself. When she made wishes on pennies and shooting stars, she never used up the wishes on herself; she always wished for a better world. When she filled all my nervous silences with jokes, I knew she had already taken hold of my heartstrings.

Aleena was the first woman I ever seriously dated, and every physical milestone with her felt monumental. We spent hours talking in my car before our first kiss. We brushed each other's arms on dates but didn't act on it. For months, when needing to change clothes, we'd blush, then leave the room to undress privately.

So that day when we were lying in our underwear, my hands had trembled as they'd traced their way from her jeans to the skin just below her waistband. She had been nervous too—perhaps because of my inexperience. She had glanced away, avoiding my eager, anxious gaze. Soon we were draped across her velvet comforter in our underwear, seeing each other's bodies for the first time.

When Aleena realized I could see the backs of her thighs, she said, "Don't look at my stretch marks."

I looked away and then slowly looked back. After a moment, I let my finger draw along a stretch mark that zigzagged down the back of her leg. She didn't tense or pull away but looked embarrassed, as if she could no longer hide a brutal secret.

"You're so beautiful," I said. The words sounded clichéd. I wished I had said something better. I knew an adjective as simple as *beautiful* couldn't erase all the times Aleena had been told her body was wrong.

She nodded, but I could sense her lingering discomfort. We snuggled a little longer and tried to force ourselves to relax. I breathed and eased into our closeness.

After a few minutes of our cuddling, her phone buzzed. She picked it up to check Snapchat, and that's what led to our interaction on the memories feature, with her staring at her former self, both of us haunted by our experiences with smaller bodies. Despite years of working to overcome my disappointment with my own body, I wasn't sure what to tell Aleena to alleviate her own perceived flaws.

She was the loveliest human being I had ever seen. Her hair bounced in dark, perfect ringlets. Her eyes batted enormous lashes that caught the attention of everyone around her. Her body was athletic, feminine, and visibly strong.

I pressed myself against her, struck by her presence, and I noticed how well my own body fit with hers. We measured the same length, a petite five feet three. Our legs mirrored each other. If our thighs had not been different shades of skin, we probably wouldn't have been able to tell them apart. Our bellies curled identically, and our sides folded in unison.

I had always known Aleena and I were similarly sized, but as we lay there in our underwear, I saw it with much greater clarity. Her body was so breathtakingly gorgeous, I hadn't even considered how much it was like my own. On her body, I saw how ridiculous it was to wish for a gap between the thighs. I saw how much of a waste it was to want hip bones that poked out. She had so many of the same features I hated in myself, but on her I found them stunning.

I took her phone and held up the old Snapchat photo that had upset her.

"I don't look like this," I said.

"No, but—" she said.

"My body looks so much like yours does now," I said. I pointed to a mirror across from her bed. She looked at the way our stomachs curved, and she inevitably noticed how our legs stretched across the same length of space. She couldn't argue with me.

"Do you think I should be smaller?" I said.

"No! Obviously not."

"Then you can't hate your body," I said. "It looks just like mine."

We stared at our strange, similar selves in the mirror. Suddenly we did not feel so vulnerable in our underwear-clad bodies. Our shoulders released a tension we had been carrying since we'd begun undressing. Aleena moved my hand to her thigh, where I had previously traced the lines of her stretch marks.

We weren't cured of our insecurities that day. Sometimes social media will remind me of my thinner days, showing me photos of myself when my collarbones protruded or when there was a gap between my thighs, a light shining through the space I had carved out of myself.

The pictures don't bother me much anymore because, more often, photos appear on my feed of Aleena and me snuggled together in our sports bras. Our tummies curl. Our cheeks are full. And I know that behind these photos are ice cream dates and evenings spent cooking pasta in the kitchen and weekend bottles of wine poured late into the night.

We no longer wish for our sculpted bodies. It has become hypocritical to hate ourselves while loving each other. As much as falling for Aleena has been a love story between the two of us, falling for her has also been a love story between my mind and my body, which, after years of turmoil, have finally learned to make peace with one another.

30

Like a Lady

Joe and I arrived at the Denver airport late in the afternoon. We were headed to a competition in Germany. It was one of our most important events yet. Ice dancers from nearly twenty countries would be attending, and with the Olympics scheduled later in the season, the competition came with higher stakes. Joe and I weren't exactly in the running for an Olympic slot, but we hoped to bring our international scores closer to those of the U.S. skaters who were being considered as Olympic alternates.

A few days before leaving for the competition, I had broken my nose. Near the end of a long practice session, Joe had taken my hand and spun me toward his body while we ran through our rumba program. We both gave the twirl a little more energy than usual, and as my ponytail whipped through the air, my face collided with Joe's forehead. I heard a crunch. The collision resulted in a killer headache, and my nose permanently shifted itself a few degrees to the right, but I still showed up to practice the very next day, relatively unshaken.

I tried not to let the injury stifle my excitement for our upcoming competition. I had never been to Europe, and the fact that I was being sent there as a part of Team USA gave me goose bumps. The competition was scheduled to take place at an ice rink that some of my friends had described as the prettiest in the world, so I ignored the pain between my eyelids and coasted on the endorphins of my precompetition high.

At the airport, Joe and I met up with several adults who would be accompanying us on our trip—judges and coaches and team coordinators who would make sure the athletes were taken care of along the way. We checked our suitcases and proceeded toward the security line.

As we walked, one of the adults stopped me.

"You really need to learn to walk more like a lady," she said. Then she mimicked my gate, offering up an unsolicited demonstration. Her impression was not flattering: She lumbered with every step like a boyish yeti.

I rolled my eyes.

"I don't see why you have to criticize the way I walk," I

said dryly. The bridge of my nose throbbed, and I wasn't in the mood for scrutiny.

"It matters," she said. "Judges from other countries will see you walking around at the competition. And the way you move your body off the ice affects the way you move your body on the ice."

Joe gave me a look that said, *Just ignore her.*

But it was hard to ignore the message I was being sent: People in the skating world cared about my walk. They cared about my femininity. They wanted to see someone sylphlike and delicate—not just on the ice, but at *all times.* And for a moment, it didn't seem to matter that I was someone with grit and perseverance . . . someone who had traveled across the country as a teenager to make my dreams a reality, someone who loved skating more than anything else on earth. It didn't seem to matter that I was someone who hardly ever missed practices, not even for painful injuries. It didn't seem to matter that I had an excitement for skating—an excitement so fierce, I got goose bumps on the way to every international competition.

Skating didn't love me back. When was I going to understand?

I was a joke. A failure in proper femininity. Even though I knew that my walk shouldn't matter, I couldn't let the criticism go.

As we continued toward the security line, I walked on

the balls of my feet. I made sure my shoulders held completely still. I swayed my hips in ultrawomanly waves.

I did what was expected of me.

When we arrived in Germany, I only texted Aleena when the coast was completely clear. I banished my love to the back of my own mind. I kept playing the same part I had been playing my whole life.

For some reason, I still cared about scoring well at my competitions. I still thought that maybe someday all my sacrifices would be worth it. Or at least that's what I told myself.

In the end, my acting didn't really matter.

Joe and I had two really rough skates while we were in Germany, and all my efforts to be more ladylike suddenly seemed like a waste of time.

31

The Makeover Scene

In an effort to start feeling more comfortable with my sexuality, I played with my style.

As soon as I got back from the competition in Germany, I wandered into the men's section of a clothing store and tabbed along the hangers of button-up shirts. My hands meandered through navy blues and forest greens. The fabrics had been pressed firm and neat. The shoulders cornered sharply. The difference between the men's section and the women's section seemed to lie mostly in colors and angles: Sharp, moody torsos replaced the liquid-pastel crops that flourished inside the designated female half of the store.

The truth is, I had always loved the lavishness of the women's section. Growing up with an older brother, I had worn his hand-me-downs throughout childhood. I knew the comfort of a plain cotton tee and the delightful shapelessness of a baggy pair of sweats, but I had still always preferred distinctly girly attire. I liked glitter and dresses and skirts and silky bras and every shade of pink.

I was a figure skater, after all.

But I had begun to question: Would my sexuality make more sense to me (and to everyone else) if I changed things up? If I started appearing different on the outside, could I communicate the change that had blossomed inside me?

Maybe I wouldn't have to go through the ordeal of coming out to the whole world if I just slowly started *looking gay*. . . .

I wouldn't dare experiment with my appearance at the ice rink, but everywhere else, I tried leaning into my queerness. I wanted a transformation just like all the makeover scenes in teen movies: I wanted the glamour of a *Princess Diaries* or *Clueless* type of reveal. Except instead of removing my glasses and putting on some eyeliner, I wanted someone to spin me around in a swivel chair and unveil a hot, undeniable lesbian: the kind of woman who made other women question themselves. Since I didn't have a makeover crew on hand, I resolved to take on the transformation myself.

I figured that a good place to start was the button-up

section of the men's department. At least, that was what my continued Google searches of the words *lesbian fashion* seemed to suggest. The more I scrolled through images of women in rolled sleeves and cuffed jeans, the more drawn I felt to the aesthetic.

I snuck a couple of shirts underneath my arms and wandered back to the women's dressing room, trying not to raise any suspicion. In my conservative Colorado neighborhood, the act of trying on men's shirts felt nearly forbidden, and I silently hoped I wouldn't be stopped by any dressing-room attendants. I didn't want to be forced to answer any questions they might have had. I didn't want to face any curious looks. I was still afraid of taking too many creative liberties with my appearance. I was still afraid of bending the world's unspoken rules.

Queer bodies are risky. It is radical to live in a body that asserts its difference. From the moment we are born, we are raised to stay in our lanes, and to cut ourselves into halves, and to shop in only one section of the store. Choosing to question these lessons is a kind of rebellion.

When I walked into the dressing room, I was afraid— but alongside my fear, I felt an untangling of my veins. A brilliant rush.

On a rack directly beside the women's dressing room, a floral dress caught my eye. I couldn't stop myself from feeling its fabric between my fingers. I picked up the hanger and swung the dress's frolicking skirt. I had been determined to stick with items from the men's section—this was meant to be a makeover, after all—but I couldn't help myself. I hastily stacked the floral dress atop my other finds.

In the changing room, I tried on the button-up shirts first. I buttoned the collars all the way up my neck and posed in the mirror. I crossed and uncrossed my arms. I placed my hands on my hips. I made serious faces. I tried to take a couple of selfies documenting my awkward poses, but I quickly deleted every picture.

I look just like my brothers, I thought, a little disheartened.

After giving up on the shirts, I tried on the dress. I spun around, letting the skirt coast on the breeze of my spinning. The fabric floated gravityless while I twirled. And I frowned, because I didn't feel comfortable as this person anymore either—I no longer wanted to be this twirling, flowery, straight-seeming girl.

I didn't end up buying the dress or the button-up shirts. I walked back to my car empty-handed.

I drove home feeling like I no longer belonged to the world. Like I was a soul drifter—never quite comfortable in my commitments, never assured enough in my sense of self to actually choose what kind of person I wanted to be.

Aleena mostly giggled at my efforts to reinvent myself.

She had a closet full of button-ups and rolled-sleeved shirts and hoodies that she had collected over time. Her style came naturally. Her wardrobe was effortlessly cool and undeniably gay, and I was jealous.

One morning, around Christmastime, I left a heap of Aleena's shirts on the floor of her bedroom. I tested out her clothes on my own body—trying to superimpose her comfortable queerness onto myself.

"Please tell me you're going to hang those up when you're done," she said. She was still lying in bed. I blew her a kiss from across the room.

"Of course," I said. "Just give me a few minutes. . . ."

I slid another one of her shirts off its hanger—a pink collared shirt with little cacti stitched into the chest. I cherished the tender familiarity of the color. When I finished dressing, I reached my arms out to the side.

"How do I look?" I asked.

Aleena couldn't stifle a laugh. "This just isn't you!" she tried to explain. "You're a femme. A lipstick lesbian . . . or, I guess, technically a lipstick *bisexual.*"

I sighed. I knew there were words for women like me— queer women who didn't generally want to give up glitter and mascara—but I still didn't know many of these women in real life, so hearing the words felt like listening to a foreign language. I couldn't quite grasp their meaning or their significance.

"Right now, nobody can even tell that I'm gay at all," I complained.

Aleena got out of bed and walked toward me. She hooked her arms around my waist. Then her lips bent into a mischievous grin.

"If you want people to know that you're gay," she said, "all you have to do is kiss me over and over and over again in public."

Then she brought her lips to mine and began unbuttoning the shirt I had just put on. I slid the square-shouldered sleeves off my arms and threw the shirt toward the pile of other failed outfits on the floor.

I got my hair cut on Valentine's Day: a gift of love to myself.

Joe and I had just returned from competing at the national championships. Although we skated fairly well, we had placed ninth—our lowest placement ever at the senior level. The Olympic team was named, and we felt distanced from the entire occasion. Even though we were among the top ten teams in the nation, we were disappointed and unsure of what the next steps in our career would be. Would it be worth it to keep going? Did figure skating have a place for us anymore?

By the time we made our way back home, we were looking for strategies to cheer ourselves up.

For years, I had been saying I wanted a pixie cut, but mostly, I spoke about short hair with the same kind of wistful inflection people use to talk about their childhood dreams of visiting Mars or digging tunnels to the center of the earth. That is to say, I never really planned on cutting my hair. I liked the idea of cutting my hair, I liked the dream of it, but I didn't necessarily plan on taking any real action. Cutting my hair would be a bold move in the world of ice dance, where choreography abounds with hair flips, and female skaters are typically seen with flowing, shiny tresses.

Plus, every time I brought up the prospect of pixie cuts in conversation, I was met with resistance: *Not all women can pull it off, you know. You'll miss your long hair after a couple of weeks. And besides, what will the judges think?*

But as my efforts to reinvent my style failed again and again, I decided I needed to ignore all the warnings. And I was really tired of worrying about what the judges thought. I didn't want to care about judges' opinions anymore.

I sat in the salon chair and offered pictures of Carey Mulligan to my beloved hairdresser, Bianca. She swiped through my phone, looking at the images and trying to piece together how she could make Carey's pixie cut flatter my haphazard brunette spirals.

Bianca worked slowly. She trimmed here and there. She ran her nails against my scalp. My foot tapped relentlessly against the floor. My frantic energy clearly made Bianca nervous.

"Are you sure you're ready for this?" she asked me before bringing a buzzing razor to the back of my head.

"I've wanted this since I was a kid," I said. "Go for it."

Then I watched my tresses peel onto the floor, falling from the sky like feathers.

About an hour passed.

When I spun around in the swivel chair, I had to feign delight as best I could. I didn't want to hurt Bianca's feelings. She had been so careful; she had done her best.

But I wanted to cry.

My face looked completely different from the face I had always known. My features seemed more pronounced. More peculiar and offensive. *How did I fail to notice how strangely my head is shaped?* I thought.

On the drive to Aleena's apartment, I could hardly bear to look in the rearview mirror, so I tried not to make any abrupt lane changes.

It was still Valentine's Day—the first Valentine's Day Aleena and I were spending together—but I no longer felt like celebrating. When I got to the parking lot of her apartment, I sat in my car and let the stereo play a rotation of indie sad girls: Julien Baker, Mitski, Soccer Mommy. I closed my eyes and disappeared into their mourning voices. I wanted to sit in my car forever. Stepping outside meant facing the world without a curtain of hair to hide behind. It meant abandoning a certain kind of femininity that held comfort and respect and ease. I didn't want Aleena to see me, but eventually my phone vibrated from the arrival of a text.

Are you on your way yet? Aleena asked. *I miss you!* she added.

Just parked! Walking upstairs now! I answered.

When I opened the door to her apartment, Aleena let out a theatrical gasp. I frowned.

"I know it looks weird," I said.

"No, it looks great!" she insisted, but her voice was a pitch too high.

Aleena stopped talking, and she pulled my body toward hers. Pressed to me, she gently let her hands slide up the back of my neck. She ran her fingers along the fuzz at the base of my skull, exploring the new sensation. Then she ruffled the half curls that remained at the top of my head.

"I actually really like it," she said, this time more convincingly.

I moved to her kitchen table and waited while she finished plating the extravagant dinner she had made. She wasn't exactly a practiced chef, but she had spent hours carefully following recipes to give us a special night. There were braised pork chops and golden mashed potatoes. There was a fancy foreign bottle of wine.

Right as Aleena was about to bring me a set of silverware, something exploded in the kitchen. Shards of glass sparkled through the sky. A knife shot across the room. I caught a glimpse of blood streaking along Aleena's arm.

A glass pan had accidentally been left on top of the stove, and the rising heat caused the pan to explode. In a matter of seconds, there were shards in the mashed potatoes, shards in the pork chops, shards in the crevices of tile beneath our bare feet.

We were lucky nobody got seriously hurt. Aleena walked away with only a minor scratch. I wasn't injured at all.

We spent the rest of the evening picking up the fractured pieces, standing on top of glass, hoping we didn't take a wrong step, but we kept laughing the entire time. I felt strangely safe. Like these footsteps were the least careful footsteps of my entire life. Like I was finally living wholly. I had cut my hair. I was at my girlfriend's apartment. I had gained a story to tell. I wasn't holding myself back anymore. I wasn't living just to win medals and get ahead. I kept thinking, *I'm having fun,* but this time, the thought didn't feel forced or fleeting. It felt honest.

After nearly two hours of cleaning the kitchen, Aleena and I retreated to her bedroom. We spooned beneath her covers. She continued to tousle the sheared waves of my hair. She placed her nose right up against mine. And I felt gay, and alive, and full.

The next morning, I put on one of my favorite dresses. I traced lip gloss over my lips, and I mascaraed my lashes, and I sprayed Aleena's cologne along the curve of my neck. My hair was still sprawling from sleep—it reminded me of the boy-band crushes I had in high school.

And when I turned around in the mirror, I looked like a mix of everything and everyone I had ever loved. And I liked the person I saw.

32

A Small Love Letter

Joe and I decided that the 2019 season would be our chance to shake up the skating world. We knew we would have to prepare a tango for our rhythm dance, but for the free dance, we wanted to do something bold. Something new. For the first time in our lives, we wouldn't care so much about our scores.

First we had to pick the right piece of music to skate to.

Choosing the program music is one of the most important aspects of the season for all skaters. Teams can spend weeks listening to playlists. Sometimes the perfect song falls into place, and sometimes the decision stirs up intense debate. Everyone has to agree: coaches, choreographers, athletes.

Months after returning from nationals, Joe and I still hadn't settled on the perfect song. We knew we had to pick something special. We wanted to select a piece that represented our personalities—a piece that showcased our collective queerness and our rebellious attitudes. Joe had supported me since I first began questioning my sexuality. We had spent many weekend mornings sitting at local brunch spots, comparing our similar but variant queer experiences in the skating world. Since Joe had been out for several years already, he held my hand and offered me words of wisdom. We could feel that our partnership was something precious and unique. As far as we knew, there had never been another internationally ranked team with two queer partners. After so many seasons of trying to fit into the right boxes, and after so many seasons of trying to do what we thought the judges would like best, we wanted to create a program that brought something completely different to the table.

Besides, after our ninth-place finish at nationals, what did we have to lose?

I suggested a Mary Lambert spoken-word poem with lyrics about falling in love with a woman. Joe suggested a melancholy song about the end of the world. One of our coaches offered a brassy piece full of trumpets and snare drums.

We fought for hours over the options.

Then one of our choreographers showed up at the rink. He had been working on a TV show in London and was eager to see the progress we had made while he was away.

"We actually don't have anything yet," we confessed. "We can't agree on music for our free dance."

"Hmm." He paused. He scrolled through his phone for a minute, and then he plugged it into the rink's speakers. "How about this?"

The speakers played a version of the 1980s pop song "Sweet Dreams (Are Made of This)." Joe and I immediately started dancing. Then the beat dropped, and we started dancing some more.

"This is perfect!" one of our coaches said.

And it was.

The song felt like a celebration. A party. A nightclub.

After practice, we brought the song to one of our dance teachers, and we played around with the music off ice. It wasn't long before our dance teacher was voguing—a dance style that originated in queer spaces, a dance style that was birthed by Black and Latinx people, a dance style that was subversive and imaginative and revolutionary.

We knew we would have to incorporate voguing into our program somehow. We knew our program had to exist as a small love letter to LGBTQ+ history. Our program would be a thank-you to the drag queens, and the activists, and the just-discovering-themselves queer kids.

Our program would be a sweet dream.

The skating world could be very stifling, but we were going to create a performance that wasn't.

33

Coming Out to Everyone

In June, I made a promise.

It all started when Aleena had a day off from work. She wanted to tag along to one of my skating practices. My training days had been especially daunting—Joe and I were vying for a spot at Skate America, which could potentially be the biggest competition of our lives. After the 2018 Olympics, several teams had retired, and Joe and I saw the new season as our chance to move up in the ranks. Skate America could be our first assignment on the Grand Prix circuit—one of the highest forms of international competition outside the world championships and Olympic Games. Basically, being in the running for a spot at

Skate America meant that we might finally get a shot at joining the big leagues.

We had been staying at the rink longer than usual, and we were often exhausted by the time we returned home in the evenings. Aleena figured that coming to the rink might be the only way she could spend time with me.

"You'll be bored," I told her. "We just do the same elements over and over for like five hours. It's honestly even boring for *me* sometimes."

"I'll be bored at home. I want to come," she insisted.

I sighed and bit the edge of my lip.

"Just tell the truth. You don't want me to come because you don't want people at the rink to ask about me?"

I didn't answer, but Aleena was right. After an entire year of dating, I had become an expert at hiding our relationship. My closest circle knew about her, but I hid my queerness from just about everyone else—especially everyone at the local ice rinks. I told myself I was just trying to protect us both.

"I hate lying," I said. "If I bring you to the rink, people are going to ask about you, and I'm sick of telling people that you're my friend."

"Then tell them I'm your girlfriend!" Aleena said.

She started to cry. I started to cry.

Obviously, Aleena knew that things weren't so simple. We had gone through the motions of the coming-out conversation on a million other occasions. Aleena knew the skating community could be extremely critical and cruel. She knew I had a large extended family full of aunts and uncles who were not entirely familiar with *the gays*. She knew my personality well enough to understand that—generally speaking—I wasn't someone who could easily abandon my worries.

But that didn't mean Aleena ever stopped hoping I would come to my senses and realize that a life of hiding wasn't the kind of life that either of us deserved.

"Don't cry," she said. "I just want to be allowed in. I want to come to your skating competitions, and I want to meet your family. Sometimes being with you feels like being in the closet all over again."

"I know," I replied. "I'm sorry."

We stared at each other for a while. I was running late for practice, but I couldn't bring myself to leave. We stood inside a dewy paralysis—unable to take a step toward each other and unable to take a step toward the door.

"Go to practice, babe," she finally said. "I'll see you when you get back."

"What if I make you a deal?" I suggested. "If Joe and I are offered a spot at Skate America, I want you to be there in the stands. I want the first skating event you ever attend to be the competition that means the most to me."

A few weeks later, Joe and I received the good news: All our grueling practices had been worthwhile. We got a call from the offices at U.S. Figure Skating. We had been chosen to compete at Skate America.

After I got the news, I immediately presented Aleena with a poem I had written—a kind of thank-you note, apology, invitation, and love letter all wrapped in a package of metaphors and rhyme. I emailed her the poem while she was at work. The subject line read: *Come with me to Skate America?*

I waited for hours to receive a response, but the whole day passed, and no reply arrived in my inbox. When Aleena finally showed up at my apartment in the evening, she admitted that she had not read the email yet.

"I want you to read it aloud to me," she said.

And so I did.

My voice floated through a story of our relationship—wavering and crackling every inch of the way. I read lines about fear, and patience, and shame, and release. I felt the panic creeping into my throat, but I pushed back against its weight.

I owed myself some air.

I had been holding on to so much guilt for not being out, but somehow, I was still finding ways to turn my fear into art. I was still finding ways to write love poems through my shame. That had to count for something.

Once I was done, I looked up at Aleena.

"I can't wait to come to Skate America," she said.

"I think this is how I'm going to come out to everyone," I said. "I'm going to read this poem."

In the following weeks, Aleena and I found a community poetry group.

The group hosted open mics at a public library on Saturday nights, and Aleena and I showed up, tentative, holding hands. I brought my notebook, and Aleena brought her guitar, and we practiced performing my poem together for a small crowd of strangers. (Aleena is a really great musician, and she came up with the idea of singing a cover of a love song between my poem's lines.)

The audiences at the library were small and eclectic. We met high schoolers who were looking for a space to be themselves, and thirty-something couples who were looking to connect, and retired English professors who sat in the back and snapped for all the performers.

When Aleena and I took the stage together, my mouth went dry. If I had closed my eyes, I could have believed I was taking the ice at a competition; I could have believed the smattering of folding chairs had turned into a packed set of bleachers and the library's ceiling had transformed into the open rafters of an arena.

I adjusted the mic and took a deep breath. Aleena strummed. The crowd of friendly faces nodded, as if to say, *Keep going.* I opened my mouth, and for a single second, I feared that no sound would escape—but in that painful second of silence, Aleena kept strumming, and her hypnotic sounds soothed my fears. I carried on. I spoke my secrets to a small room of strangers—my words found their way into the air. And when I finished, I was met with the sound of castanets. The holy snapping of fingers.

And if I had closed my eyes, I could have believed that I was ending a program. I could have believed that an entire arena full of people was clapping for me.

Two weeks before Skate America, I sat cross-legged on Aleena's bed; Aleena sat next to me, holding her guitar. Fairy lights hung from her ceiling. We looked comfortable, peaceful.

We hit the record button of her camera.

When I watch the video now, I'm surprised at how confident I managed to appear. In reality, I felt exposed, like I was handing over my phone to a stranger—a thousand strangers—and letting them scroll through every photo and text and note I'd ever saved, but I managed to give off a reasonable impression of calmness.

I guess skating taught me to fake bravery well.

Aleena played the love song, and between her notes, I spoke the words of the poem I had written for her. The poem went like this:

I've been with you for a whole year,
and I wanted to say
thank you.
Mostly, thank you
for being here
even though I've made your love
my shadow.
I have nudged you to
stay in the dark and gray
when we both know
you are someone who has
light bursting from your belly.

Thank you for waiting
through every conversation
that I've referred to you as my best friend,
not because you are not
my best friend (you are),
but because I've had to swallow
the words
my love, my love, my love
each time instead.

Thank you for turning
a cheek to the times
I have turned mine—
the moments public displays of affection
made me feel naked,

the times I let the grip
of a held hand slip
into the fear of being found out.
I know how much it has hurt you
that I have not been able to be completely out.
I know it's been a blow
with every missed invitation and holiday gone by,
every picture posted with
you missing from my side.
Every time I've answered that No,
I'm not seeing anyone,
when I wish I could say that I am
finally doing more than just seeing.
What a limited sense
to describe being with you. I am glowing.
I am whole.
I am so completely new.

I have dragged you back
into the closet with me.
And we both know closet
is much too kind a metaphor.
Call it a prison cell,
call it a lifelong panic attack,
call it being buried alive,
call it the nightmares I still get sometimes.
The ones where

everyone who wouldn't approve
suddenly shows up as I'm kissing you.
There is no pretty way to say
that I've made myself sick
living my life this afraid.
I have spent the past year
as two different people,
bags under each of their eyes
for different reasons—
neither side of the pillow feels safe.
I grow more exhausted each day.
I keep shelling this sand in my stomach
and praying the pain turns into a pearl.
I am itching to shed my skin.
I have long outgrown the cocoon.
Why do we only let animals emerge
from the winter
as something brand-new?
Up to this point has been a hibernation.
Today I am waking with the biggest yawn,
stretching my limbs, and saying,
I'm Karina—
it's nice to meet you after so long.

At the end of the day,
secrets have only made me sad.
I am finally more scared

of living this way forever
than I am of letting people know
who I am.

Darling, come to the family reunions.
Show up for my events at work.
Kiss me on the cheek
while walking our city's busiest sidewalk.
I won't even stop to see who is there.
A year ago, I got to meet you.
One year later,
everyone else gets to meet me too.
From now on,
I'll walk into every room smiling,
parting the crowd,
making my way through.
I'll make sure they know I'm here.

I'll make sure they know I'm with you.

We practiced our duet over and over again, but we found flaws in every take. We bickered over little details. In one recording, my voice sounded too quiet. In another, Aleena stumbled through a few chords on her guitar.

We were both nervous. I was about to reveal our long-hidden relationship to the entire social-media-consuming world.

The moment elicited rational worries. I feared how the

skating world would react. No female skater had ever come out while competing on the international circuit, and coming out would mean offering myself up to the unknown. I felt nervous about how people would perceive a team with not only one but two queer athletes. Would judges make snide comments? Would other athletes stop making eye contact with me in the locker rooms? I feared how some of my extended family members' perceptions of me would change. I feared the barrage of stereotypes and insults that threatened to follow me out of the closet. Aleena and I both worried about how our relationship would shift once our romance was pushed out of the shadows I had created to conceal it.

But I actually had a bigger fear. A fear of letting go. I'd spent so many years uncomfortable with myself that I wasn't sure how to live openly. I didn't know how to survive without secrets and restraint. So much of my existence had been a series of small, quiet shames held close to my chest—but I was finally beginning to understand the gravity and importance of moving beyond my own silence. I finally understood that some stories needed to live outside my own body.

I sat on Aleena's bed, and I uploaded the video to all my social media accounts. Then I put my phone down, and I went to sleep.

By the next morning, my secret had spread. It wasn't a secret anymore.

When Joe and I took the ice at Skate America, my family members sat in the stands and Aleena sat beside them.

Our names were announced alongside the words *Representing the United States of America*. . . . We skated toward the center of the ice, and I looked out into the audience. Just as my eyes lifted toward the crowd, I saw a half dozen rainbow flags blooming throughout the arena. I saw pockets of color waving, and billowing, and dancing.

And I thought those flags looked like souls set free. I wished I had seen the image of all those flags when I was writing my coming-out poem, because they were better than anything that I could have ever imagined.

That's what happens when we let our stories live outside our bodies: They take on a vibrant life of their own.

34

The Sweetest Dream

Despite the elation of competing at Skate America, and the fact that our programs were celebrated by the crowds, and the fact that I was finally out and proud, the remainder of my last competitive season was fraught with stress.

Joe and I knew that the upcoming nationals would probably be our final competition.

We didn't receive very much funding from U.S. Figure Skating for the season, and our parents couldn't help support us financially anymore. After years of taking on debt in order to help pay for my training, my parents had spread themselves too thin, and they didn't have anything left to offer me. For years, they had tried not to show signs of the financial strain I had caused. They had tried to make it seem like my life as an athlete was not a burden—but after contributing to a seventeen-year skating career, my parents had been wrung entirely dry.

Ever since we were teenagers, Joe and I had been working part-time jobs whenever we weren't at the rink, but our jobs couldn't provide nearly enough to cover the fees for equipment and ice time and costumes and choreography and coaching. The only reason we were able to compete in our final season at all was that several of our coaches generously offered to help us out—discounting our training costs and sacrificing their own income.

But still, the lack of funding added a layer of anxiety. My skates were duct-taped together. I was often sleep-deprived because I took on extra shifts at my job. I tried selling my old clothes at consignment stores so I could keep attending dance classes. I constantly offered to house-sit and babysit on weekends so I could keep getting my blades sharpened. Every minute I wasn't training, I was trying to come up with new ways to afford training.

The pressure leaked into practices.

I found myself arguing with Joe without completely understanding why. Both of us broke into fits of tears while we sashayed and twizzled through our programs. We spent a lot of time hardly speaking to one another at all. Most days, we circled the rink in silence, holding hands with slightly too tight a grip.

One morning, a few minutes after taking the ice, Joe and I caught blades on a simple crossover circle, and we both slid into the boards. A resounding boom echoed over the arena. Joe's body tangled with mine. My leggings dampened from the layer of water that had been left by the Zamboni. By the time Joe and I got back on our feet, we were already snapping at one another, trying to pass the blame. If we had not been under so much stress, we probably would have stood up laughing, but our normal sense of comradery had slowly diminished. We never seemed to be in the mood for jokes anymore.

One of our choreographers noticed that we were bickering, and she told us to take a break and sort things out, so Joe and I got off the ice, unlaced our skates, and sat together at the top of the bleachers. For a long time, we didn't speak. We let anger ferment the cold air between our bodies. We watched the other skaters continue to practice—they seemed so eager, so packed with potential. In their world, every dream was still possible. In their world, skating still held an unpredictable and exciting future. But in our world, a lifetime's worth of ambition was disappearing before our very eyes.

For the first time in my existence, I didn't want to confront an ending. I didn't want to see the spoilers. Even though I was only twenty-two, I felt acutely old. Knowing nationals was going to be my last competition felt like finding out the exact moment that I would die.

"What's wrong with us?" Joe asked.

"I can't stop thinking about how this is all going to be over soon," I said.

"I know," Joe said. "All we can do it make the most of these last couple of weeks."

We hugged. We didn't talk anymore. We just held one another.

Then we got back onto the ice. We clutched at an unspoken belief: If things had to end, maybe they could end in fireworks.

～

Nationals took place in Detroit that year, and getting to Detroit seemed like it might be the hardest part of the competition.

A winter storm blew across the Great Lakes region, and our plane was rerouted in midair. I had been sleeping when the pilot announced to passengers that because of the inclement weather, we would be landing at a different airfield. However, my sleep-weary ears chose to hear that our plane would be landing in a *field*.

Flying has always given me a sense of unease. Any slight disturbance midair is enough to send my nervous system into disarray, but this was more than just a slight disturbance.

Cue panic.

Cue my frantic, unreliable heartbeats.

Turbulence caused the suitcases above our heads to rattle in their bins. I imagined the plane torpedoing toward the earth like a cursed meteor shower raining down on a meadow. Hadn't I wished to end in fireworks? I silently wondered if I had brought this fate upon myself; if maybe my own thoughts had somehow bent my life into a tragic shape. I clung to an armrest as if my grip could cushion the inevitable blow. *Maybe I will have a heart attack before we hit the ground,* I thought.

Luckily, another skater was sitting next to me, and he noticed my sweaty palms.

"Are you all right?" he asked.

"Why aren't *you* scared? We're landing in a field!" I replied. I looked around the plane. Everyone else seemed calm in their seats. Nobody else was praying. Nobody else was gripping their armrests for dear life.

The skater next to me explained that I'd misheard the pilot's announcement, and I laughed, succumbing to the gleeful tides of relief.

While I wouldn't wish my panicky thoughts on anyone, there is always a small gift in the moment when the worst-case scenarios do not play out. I know that my anxiety will never completely disappear. No matter how much

I work through the moments of doom, there will still be days when the world looks a lot like it's ending. I'll probably always be a little scared of planes, and heart disease, and water bottles dropped into the street. That's okay. I know how to name those moments and get past them now. And besides, there is a strange elation after facing terror. There is a kind of release in recognizing that sometimes when an ending looks grim, something else might still be in store.

When we finally landed in Detroit, I felt a lightness.

Joe and I breezed through our initial practices. We joked around with our competitors while we waited for the Zamboni to clear the ice. We geared up for the first part of the competition: the rhythm dance.

The day of the event, I slipped into a tango dress, and I colored my lips red with lipstick. I laced up my skates and sat in the locker room. I listened to a podcast to try to distract myself from all my nerves.

The hallway leading up to the entrance of the ice was littered with cameras and bright lights. The smell of popcorn drifted down from the stands. As each team took their turn, a new tango song played from the booming speakers. While we waited for our turn in front of the crowd, Joe and I wandered through the underground halls of the arena. The concrete tunnels were dark and severe. Every once in a while, we passed other skaters who were decorated in twinkling costumes and dramatic makeup. Everyone seemed very serious.

"I've never thought about it before," Joe said, "but sometimes skating competitions feel like ancient Rome. Like we're about to enter the Colosseum."

We both laughed because we knew that we weren't going to be fighting to the death. We weren't going to be facing a pack of tigers. We were just figure skating. At the end of the day—after all the fanfare and drama—we were just there to have fun.

A few minutes later, Joe and I held hands and skated into the center of the rink. We performed our own tango with twitching legs and serious expressions. We hit our final pose, and we sat in the kiss and cry to hear our scores. We ended up in seventh place, and we were happy. We didn't need to win. We knew those moments in front of the crowd were good enough.

The morning of the free dance, my skate broke in the middle of our final practice. One of the hooks that was meant to hold my laces in place popped off my boot, and my ankle was left wobbling and unstable.

I should have seen the disaster coming. My skates had been broken down for ages, but I ignored the signs because I knew I couldn't afford a new pair.

This can't be how my career ends, I thought.

After our practice, I sat in the locker room looking down at my ragged skates, and I let out a sigh.

Just hold up for one more program, I whispered to my boots.

I borrowed some more duct tape from another girl in the locker room, and I hoped for the best.

A few hours later, Joe and I grabbed hands and took to the ice for our final performance: the free dance.

The announcer called our names. The stands shook with more pride flags. I smiled at the section where I thought my mom and my girlfriend might be sitting. Then I crossed my legs and leaned against Joe. I slid into my starting pose: an arrogant balance on one toe pick. I narrowed my eyes into an intentional smirk.

The first musical notes began. The initial vocals were eerie. The singer twisted her vowels into a near-whisper. *Sweet dreams are made of this,* she sang.

We curled and bent to her melodies. We rolled our heads in unison. My body flung itself into our first lift. Joe and I felt completely in sync with one another. Our heart rates had somehow perfectly matched up.

The crowd settled into a focused hush.

But then, about halfway through the program, a dance

beat dropped into the song, and I bent down to my knees and slid like a rock star across the slippery ground. Joe followed behind me, and the audience couldn't hold back their cheers. The whole crowd started clapping along to the music's beat.

Joe and I followed the sound. We bobbed and ducked in time with the clapping. We soared and spun. We smiled directly at the audience. We flew across the ice. Just when the program was nearing its end, we stopped directly in front of the judges with our arms folded over our chests.

Then we vogued.

We left a little piece of queer history on the ice. We left a little piece of ourselves on the ice.

The singer let out her last lyric: *Hold your head up.*

As we hit our final pose, a few people stood up for us. One by one, more and more took to their feet. We looked around the stadium, and cheers were coming from all directions. Soon enough, the entire audience was giving us a standing ovation.

And maybe it wasn't the Olympics, and maybe it wasn't a gold-medal performance or even a podium-worthy performance, and maybe Joe and I would never be written into any record books.

But if my competitive skating career had to see an ending, that moment was the best ending I could have ever asked for.

35

The Prettiest I've Ever Felt

It happened one Monday night in the middle of February, right after Joe and I returned from nationals. There was a box of cheap blue hair dye that had been sitting in my bathroom cupboard for three weeks, and at eleven-fifteen, I felt the impulse to finally open it. My hair was already platinum blond. A judge had asked me to dye it during the competitive season because they thought the blond made me stand out on the ice, but this time, I wasn't dyeing my hair for a skating judge. I was dyeing my hair for myself.

Aleena sat on the couch watching a bad reality-TV show, and I sat on the floor between her feet.

"We're going to dye my hair," I told her.

"Isn't it a little late for that? Can't it wait until tomorrow?" she asked.

"No," I said, and I stood up to grab the dye from the cupboard.

It smelled rancid and a little too sugary—like candy left in a hot car. We held our breath and worked the mixture into my scalp, making a mess, not bothering to clean it up. My forehead freckled with blue dots. I didn't even wipe them away.

"I think it might be a little *too blue*," Aleena said, concerned. She tried to dilute the dye with conditioner. I let her play stylist while she attempted to coerce my roots into the perfect pastel shade. The reality show kept playing in the background.

After letting the dye set for a while, we rinsed it out in the sink. When I came up for air, I was surprised to see that my hair had hardly changed; my roots contained only the very faintest memory of sapphire.

"I think we diluted it too much," I said.

"I'm so tired. Let's try again tomorrow," Aleena said.

"No," I said. "I want to do this tonight."

I kissed her good night, and she went to bed.

While she slept, I dried my hair and started over. I massaged the dye back into my strands. I held my breath again. I created new blue freckles on my forehead and cheeks. The reality show ended. Nearly everyone in the apartment complex turned off their lights.

The only sounds left in the world were the late-night kind: a car door unlocking, a baby crying a few apartments away. I should have been tired, but I wasn't. I could have stayed up all night listening to the city's midnight orchestra and remembering the fact that I was alive, and I was young, and I still had time to do everything in the world that I had ever wanted to do.

I waited an hour before rinsing out the dye again. I stood in the shower and watched a turquoise puddle gather under my feet. When I was finished, I didn't even bother looking in the mirror. I liked the thought of falling asleep thinking my hair might be the color of the sky, or the color of the ocean, or the color of something vast and beautiful that I had never seen before.

36

Running Away with the Circus

Joe and I moved to Montreal in June. A few months after nationals, we got a call from casting at Cirque du Soleil. They were looking for an ice-dance couple to fill a role on a new show that they were in the process of creating.

The opportunity felt meant to be. We *really* couldn't afford competing anymore, and the job offer would mean a steady income and a chance to continue doing what we loved. (And the company would pay for me to get a new pair of skates!)

The Montreal summer was breezy. The air smelled like grass and rain. We lived in an artists' residence next to Cirque's headquarters, and the rooms had big windows and little kitchenettes. Aleena often sent me flowers and love notes, both of which I kept on the desk in the corner of my room.

I lived across the hall from Joe, and we spent most nights sitting on one another's beds, eating delivery Thai food and chatting about Joe's crushes on boys. Then we spent our mornings renting bicycles and riding them to brunch.

I felt a kind of release. Leaving the competitive-skating world behind felt like waking up from a strange dream— I couldn't remember if it was entirely good or bad, but I still held on to the relief of knowing it wasn't real anymore. I could move on.

Our entire circus cast lived together in the residence building, and the experience was exactly how I had always imagined the circus to be. Acrobats did handstands in the hallways. Musicians strummed their guitars on the patio. A juggler made a show of tossing our belongings into the air. We learned so many party tricks. We taught one another how to swear in a dozen different languages. We shared recipes and jokes. Some evenings, after long hours of rehearsals, we met in the lobby to play board games and order greasy pizzas and drink canned wine. The whole spectacle felt like summer camp for grown-ups.

We were all misunderstood-artist types—an eclectic collection of contradictory strangers from all over the world—yet somehow, we fit together like yard-sale furniture that had finally found a home.

One Saturday, we spent a grueling day training for a new act. The routine involved artists who bungee-jumped from a trapeze—flipping and careening and catching one another in the air—all while skaters danced underneath. The act was every bit as glorious and dangerous as it sounds, and if it went well, we knew the crowds would be awestruck. We spent hours perfecting our craft so we could replicate the show in arenas around the world.

When we returned home from the rehearsal, we were exhausted. Creating magic took work, but somehow, after unlacing our skates and leaving the rink, we all agreed that the night held a little more potential. We weren't quite done making magic yet.

We showered off the day's sweat. Everyone dressed up in their best shirts and their favorite pairs of skinny jeans. I wore a spaghetti-strapped crop, and the lace of my bra peeked out from its edges. I put on bright lipstick and heels. My hair was slick with pomade. My neck was soft with cologne.

We were going out.

A fellow cast member from Montreal knew of the coolest gay club—a pulsing building downtown with multiple floors and the promise of a hundred dancing bodies on any given Saturday night.

Our group filled the seats of several Ubers, and we tried to speak in broken French to our drivers. We only truly felt confident in our ability to say thank you—*merci, merci, merci*—so we relayed our gratitude again and again.

The entrance of the club opened onto a staircase. The hallway was dark. Our feet stuck to the floor, and if it had been quieter, I'm sure we would have heard the floorboards squish and squeak beneath us. We led one another to an open room where people were dancing—some on platforms, some pressed against the walls, some standing in line waiting to grab a drink from the bar. Anthems blasted from the DJ's booth: Whitney, and Britney, and Christine and the Queens.

We danced with our whole bodies. It didn't matter that we were exhausted from rehearsals. Nothing could diminish the freedom of our limbs. One of my friends took off his shirt and hooked it into his belt loop. Another vogued in the center of a circle. A third grabbed my hands so we could salsa-dance. The room smelled like cranberry and perfume. The colors reminded me of light refracted off a stained-glass window. I hadn't shaved in weeks, but I didn't even think twice before flinging my arms into the air. Our bodies hazed under the strobe lights. In the blur, we couldn't tell which movements belonged to strangers and which to ourselves, and eventually I gave up trying to distinguish the edges of myself. It was silly to try to hold on to my own borders—it was silly to try to separate myself from all the other stories and beating hearts in the room.

We looked like ghosts. Moving, dissolving, tying T-shirts to our belt loops. Somewhere between the beats of one song leaking into the beats of another, I found myself trying to resist the urge to cry. And then I found myself not resisting the urge at all.

A girl with a half-shaved head looked me up and down. She winked at me before disappearing down the staircase, and I realized I was in a room full of strangers who could see me—my armpit hair, my belly, the lace of my bra—and I didn't want anyone to turn away or close their eyes. It was the opposite of a high school locker room. It was the opposite of standing on a scale. It was the opposite of restraint. It was like being in an arena the moment before my music played. Only I wasn't afraid of falling.

I had never witnessed so many queer people all in one space. There was something a little sad about it—all our storied pasts piled together; all our tender histories dumped onto a single dance floor. But there was something holy about it too. What better place to let our pain go? What better way to reconcile these bodies—these bodies that had, at times, been so hard to live inside?

We danced for what could have been hours or years. I shimmied until someone tapped me on the shoulder.

"Let's head out. Maybe grab something to eat?"

I turned to Joe, and he nodded. I took him by the hand,

and I remembered something I hadn't remembered in years.

Heaven might be a dance floor, I thought. But this time I knew for sure. Paradise was the sea of dancing bodies. The night. The lipstick. The shirtless boys. All the precious, beautiful freaks, thundering the ground with their feet. Paradise was a room full of glittering, life-shaken people and the way we still celebrated everything we could see.

EPILOGUE

Nothing Left to Spoil

I have trained as a figure skater for nearly twenty years, but somehow, I have never stumbled across the opportunity to skate on a frozen lake. So this is my dream: Someday I want to travel to Keystone, or Canyon Ferry, or Lake Louise—anywhere the water can solidify overnight, anywhere I might be able to witness the small miracle of winter transforming a watery slice of the planet into an ice rink—and then I want to skate there.

This frozen-lake daydream is an expansive and nuanced fantasy of mine. I have even thought out the details, down to the colors and the sounds. I picture myself lacing up my skates while sitting on an aging rock; I imagine gliding under a dimming sky while the wind slaps against my coat; I imagine performing to the open air with movements I've never tried before. Maybe winter birds will fly overhead. Maybe snowflakes will fall at my feet. I'll be nearly alone: just my body, my skates, and the resilient fish swimming through the icy waters below. My skates will hiccup against the bumpy surface. It will be so different from the manufactured smoothness I have spent my whole life learning to understand. The roar of arena crowds will be replaced by the aching whispers of the evening.

Of course, I will cultivate the perfect playlist for the occasion.

Maybe—amid the emptiness and the scent of pine—I will learn to love skating as easily and openly as I once did. After nearly two decades in competitive skating, some of the magic has been washed away. When I take to the ice, I often hear a broken record of criticism repeating in my head. Sometimes I can hardly move without comparing my motions to the delicate lines and lush edges of other skaters. Skating has taught me to undo all my limits. Skating has taught me to never be satisfied with myself. I adore skating, but I hate the way it can make me feel.

These days, I've been thinking about what it really means to be a competitive ice dancer. I've been asking myself a lot of questions: What does it mean to live inside a sport where our movements and our bodies are judged?

What does it mean to participate in a sport that thrives on its exclusivity? What does it mean to turn dancing into a competition? Who gets to say which movements are the best? Who gets to say which bodies are the most beautiful? How do we decide who holds all this power?

Sometimes when I watch competitive skating on TV, I feel like crying because I remember what it felt like to want something so badly; I remember what it felt like to be willing to do anything for success in my sport.

I know what so many skaters are still going through. Some skaters are still starving. Some skaters are still closeted. Some coaches are still telling their students to push past the pain of injuries. Some judges are still advising athletes to downplay parts of themselves that might stifle their scores.

But I also cry because I miss it.

In spite of everything, I miss the rush of competition and the roar of the crowds. I miss the daily toil of training, and the incomparable feeling of waiting for my placement to be announced in the kiss and cry. Even after confronting all of my sport's shortcomings, I cannot let go of skating. I can't allow its icy hold to slip from my thoughts. I've always had a runaway heartbeat—but no matter where I've wandered, ice rinks still feel like a home to me.

Maybe one day when I turn on my TV to watch a skating competition, I'll see more skaters like me. More queer people. More ladies with thighs that touch together. More

Latinx competitors. More anxiety-ridden humans daring to step in front of crowds.

But also, I hope to turn on the TV and see skaters who are nothing like me—because I know that somewhere in the world, a young teenager might be searching Google right now, trying to find evidence to justify their own existence, and maybe the proof isn't out there yet.

To all those people: I hope you'll become your own proof. I hope you'll realize you are a part of a legacy—even if your predecessors have been hidden or erased. I hope to google your name someday and find a hyperlink thrown out into the internet's abyss. I hope you alter our sport entirely.

If I could offer you anything in the world, I'd offer you this:

Maybe someday, you and I will meet at a frozen lake. Maybe we'll step onto the ice, and we'll skate alongside a mountain wind, and we'll let our stories go. Maybe the sport of figure skating will change a little bit, and maybe the whole world will change a little bit. Maybe this transformation will take a lot of us, and maybe it will take some time, but I really believe things will be different someday.

I've already spoiled this ending, so this shouldn't come as a surprise, but if you are someone who needs to be assured, allow me to assure you one final time: We can build a future where things will be okay in the end.

ACKNOWLEDGMENTS

I am so grateful to the publications that originally gave my work a home. *Tongue-Tied* first appeared in *riverrun,* the UCCS undergraduate literary and arts journal. *I Can't Hate My Body if I Love Hers* first appeared in the Modern Love column in the *New York Times.* Both pieces have been edited for this book.

Thank you to my incredible agent, Jessica Regel, who saw the potential for my writing so early on. Connecting with you is by far the best thing that has ever happened to me on Twitter.

Thank you to my wonderful editor, Kelly Delaney. You have been so thoughtful with my stories that I couldn't imagine them under the care of anyone else. Your input has been invaluable throughout this process.

Many thanks to the entire team at Knopf who brought the book to life: Artie Bennett, Renée Cafiero, Amy Schroeder, Jake Eldred, Jonathan Morris, Ray Shappell, and Andrea Lau. Thank you to Angelina Huang for taking the photo of me on the cover, and thanks to Kate Moross for creating the bright pink cover design of my dreams.

I'm so lucky to have had teachers who saw me, even when I sat in the very back corners of their classrooms and tried to appear invisible. Thank you to the art teachers and the English teachers, and especially thank you to my professor Sarah Treschl, who agreed to sponsor my creative writing independent study, even though I asked at the very last minute. Sarah, you always made me feel like a real writer, and I think that's why I had enough naive confidence to actually become one.

Thank you to Ashlyn Gaughan, who let me stay in her spare bedroom while I was finishing the first draft of this book. I'm sorry I didn't include any stories about you—you're still one of my favorite people in the entire world.

So many of these chapters were shaped by the events that transpired during my first year living in Colorado Springs, and I would not have survived that year if it had not been for my incredible host family. Sally, Di, Britney, and Jason, thank you all for becoming actual kin.

Thank you to Uyen Carlson for looking after me during my early teenage years when I was not that fun to be around and for teaching me life lessons alongside skating ones. Thanks to Christopher Dean for creating so many perfect programs for me and Joe. Working with you has been the privilege of a lifetime (and it's also just been a lot of fun). Thank you to the many, many other coaches, choreographers, teachers, and training mates who have nurtured me through this sport. Competitive figure skating is a cold world, but your kindness has made it much warmer.

I owe so much gratitude to all the queer skaters who came before me, to all the ones who skated alongside me, and to all the ones yet to come. Being in community with you means more than I can even express.

Thank you to Joe Johnson for holding my hand and living it all by my side.

And I am so grateful for my dear family. You all have shaped me as a human being and, in turn, shaped the creation of this book. Thank you to my wonderful aunts, uncles, cousins, and grandparents, who have been showing up to support me at my skating events for years and who have loved me as a human being outside of skating. Thank you to my brothers, Luis and Marques. Since we were little, I've just been trying to keep up with you two. I know my skating career took up more than its fair share of space and resources in our family—thanks for being really good sports about that. Thank you to my mom and dad, Luis and Karin Manta, who have supported me in every way possible. You are simply the best parents out there, and I love you both so much. Finally, I cannot fail to mention the most adored member of the Manta family: our dog, Phantom. Thanks for keeping me company while I was writing this book, bubs.

Underlined

A Community of Book Nerds & Aspiring Writers!

READ

Get book recommendations, reading lists, YA news

DISCOVER

Take quizzes, watch videos, shop merch, win prizes

CREATE

Write your own stories, enter contests, get inspired

SHARE

Connect with fellow Book Nerds and authors!

GetUnderlined.com • @GetUnderlined

Want a chance to be featured? Use #GetUnderlined on social!